What People Are Sayi[illegible]

Arianrhod

I0799651

In *Arianrhod: Celtic Goddess of Fate, Fortune and Destiny*, Kristoffer Hughes explores the mysteries of Arianrhod. She is certainly an enigma: is she just a bardic tale or embedded within the stories do we find the distant echo of a powerful Welsh goddess? By going back to primary sources and a critical examination of later commentary, Kristoffer attempts to penetrate the layers of her myth.

Modern Paganism certainly claims her as a goddess – the goddess of fate, the lady of the silver wheel, who dwells in her spiral castle, the corona borealis, all attributes derived from her name. Her appeal to a modern polytheist is easy to see – when the life-force of the land is violated, Arianrhod appears and acts with Otherworldly agency to set a whole chain of events in motion. The myth is not just a story, nor is it a literal truth: it is metaphorical, guiding us to deeper truths that cannot be put into words. Kristoffer reminds us that myths did not happen 'Once upon a time', but the time of their telling is the time that they exist. By exploring our connection with Arianrhod in the present (and the last chapter of the books suggests ways of doing this), we may initiate ourselves into her mysteries. She is the still point about which all revolves, who weaves the sacred fabric that is the eternal now.

Anna Franklin, High Priestess of the Hearth of Arianrhod, author of *The Sacred Circle Tarot, Pagans Ways Tarot, The Hearth Witch's Compendium*, and many other books on Paganism

Arianrhod has long been a shadowy and elusive figure, despite also being incredibly popular among Witches and Pagans. It always seemed the modern Neo-Pagan version of Arianrhod and the native Arianrhod were two distinct entities, with an entirely different personality and body of lore. Finally, we have a book that delves into this Goddess in depth. Kristoffer Hughes peels back the mystery behind Her, allowing us to see Arianrhod as the complex and nuanced entity She is. Via language, lore, myth, and magic this book offers the reader a chance to get to know Arianrhod viscerally, fully, and discover how her transgressive, complex nature can play a role in our lives today. A must read for any lover of Welsh mythology, Celtic polytheist, or magical practitioner.
Mhara Starling, author of *Welsh Witchcraft: A Guide to the Spirits, Lore, and Magic of Wales*

Arianrhod: Celtic Goddess of Fate, Fortune and Destiny is a significant analysis of the figure, deity, and archetype which are Arianrhod/Aranrhod. By means of skilful eloquence and enchanting narrative, Kristoffer Hughes succeeds in presenting the mythological figure to a wider audience through an appropriate contextualisation which is woven into a tapestry of modern pagan interpretation. Time and again, the volume provides key insights and raises several fruitful questions regarding the multifaceted Arianrhod/Aranrhod. Indeed, Hughes' discussion can be engaged with and appreciated by the academic, the layperson, and the believer alike, which is quite the accomplishment. Cyfrol arbennig yn wir.
Dr Gareth Evans-Jones, author of *Y Cylch* and Lecturer of Philosophy and Religion, Bangor University, North Wales, UK

Although small in stature, this book is an immense treasure trove of information about Aranrhod. Combining historical connection, folklore, myth, and a deep personal understanding,

Kristoffer, in his uniquely readable style, presents this wealth of knowledge in an easy to understand and highly accessible manner. Whether you're new to this Celtic deity or have been working with her folklore and myth for a long time, the wisdom contained within will deepen your personal relationship with Aranrhod. Moreover, Kristoffer includes some excellent practical exercises which you can incorporate into your personal practice to help connect to the nature of this Goddess. The old gods are definitely stirring in prompting Kristoffer to write this book, proving "What is remembered lives".
Lisa and Anton Stewart, authors of *Simply Wicca: A beginner's Guide to the Craft of the Wise*

Kristoffer Hughes takes a deep dive into the lore and language which surrounds Arianhrod in this outstanding addition to the *Pagan Portals* series. Rather than simply recount the tales from Welsh literature, Hughes guides us through the nuance of Welsh language, introducing us to a complex deity with much relevance to the twenty-first century. The chapter on gender and ecology is particularly revelatory. By unpicking one of the thorniest issues in Yr Mabinogi, Hughes reveals the Tynged and guides readers through ways these figures can transform our lives and our practise. Whether you are a newcomer to Celtic deities or are a long-time practitioner, there is plenty here to enrich your relationship with the spinner of the silver wheel.
Andrew Anderson, author of *The Ritual of Writing, Artio and Artaois* and *The Magic of Cats*

Hughes dives deep, covering a lot of ground and a lot of complexity in such a short tome. Whether you are new to working with Arianrhod or a lifelong devotee, this compact yet thoroughly-researched and thoughtful work will bring your relationship with the goddess to new depths.
Enfys J Book, author of *Queer Qabala* and *Queer Rites*

Kristoffer is a natural, soothing yet formidable teacher. As a person seeped in Welsh language heritage, education, history and mysteries, I believe that nobody has dived as deeply into the very depths of the mythic, linguistic and spiritual Welsh landscape like Hughes. This little book holds so much treasure and knowledge and is just bursting with Awen. An exquisite portrait of Arianrhod awaits you, one which you will be guided to find and paint within yourself through Kristoffer's exquisite writing.
Carys Eleri, author of *Dod nôl at fy nghoed* and award-winning Welsh actress, comedian, singer, composer, and TV presenter

For all those a little mystified by this enigmatic Goddess, who on the surface might appear mythically puzzling and obscure, this book is a forensic exploration of Arianrhod's central myth and character, challenging some long-held assumptions and giving back a spiritual and psychological fullness to her story. Kristoffer Hughes' insight, clarity and knowledge of primary sources – and the nuanced beauty of the Welsh language – reveals to us a deity of breadth and depth, affording us a more rounded and resonant understanding of this often-misunderstood Goddess.
Philip Carr-Gomm, author of *Druid Mysteries*

Pagan Portals

Arianrhod

Celtic Goddess of Fate,
Fortune and Destiny

Pagan Portals

Arianrhod

Celtic Goddess of Fate, Fortune and Destiny

Kristoffer Hughes

MOON BOOKS

London, UK

Washington, DC, USA

CollectiveInk

First published by Moon Books, 2025
Moon Books is an imprint of Collective Ink Ltd.,
Unit 11, Shepperton House, 89 Shepperton Road, London, N1 3DF
office@collectiveinkbooks.com
www.collectiveinkbooks.com
www.moon-books.net

For distributor details and how to order please visit the 'Ordering' section on our website.

ISBN: 978 1 80341 827 8
978 1 80341 915 2 (ebook)
Library of Congress Control Number: 2024942247

A CIP catalogue record for this book is available from the British Library.

Design: Lapiz Digital Services

UK: Printed and bound by CPI Group (UK) Ltd, Croydon, CR0 4YY
US: Printed and bound by Thomson-Shore, 7300 West Joy Road, Dexter, MI 48130

Contents

Introduction

Wyt harddwch, wyt urddas, rho i'm Aranrhod dy 'ras
(You are beauty, you are dignity, Aranrhod bestow upon me your grace)

To engage with Arianrhod is to step into a mystery that was old when the world was new. Her song is a unique fusion of deep mystery combined with socio-political and religious syncretism; she is the product of tens of thousands of story tellers that stretch impossibly through time. She is a whisper that rises from a tumultuous river whose snare encompasses the land.

For centuries academics and layman alike have strived to decode this mysterious figure whose voice cannot be silenced, whose tempestuous, non-conforming nature cannot be tamed nor held in chains. Bards have crumbled before the might of her radiance, their love songs to her peeling through the cosmos in search of connection, or a depth of spirit that transforms their songs. Lovers of mythology have scratched away at words and their shadows between the lines to discover a truth that they and occultist alike have strived to discern for generations – who is she?

It is, in essence the million-pound question, her voice rises from the pages of mythology, she sings from the triads of Britain and the poetry of the supreme Bard of Welsh culture – Taliesin. Witches, Druids, magicians and polytheists have battled with incorrect conclusion and assumption to develop a goddess suitable for modern Pagan practise, many were inspired, many have failed, and some have abandoned the cause altogether. The elusive nature of this figure is such that many will break in their search of her, she encourages a cosmic sifting of a nature that many will abandon for easier deities, less complex. But it is her complexity and her tendency to not conform that pulls at the curious spirt that compels those in search of her mystery to continue their journey to discover the nature of Arianrhod – but who is she?

She has become the weaver, the silver wheel, the light of the corona borealis – the northern crown which is said to be her abode in the starry skies. She has taken to a spinning wheel to twist and turn the silvery threads of contemporary western paganism as it found its tentative feet under the table of modern spirituality. And yet – through all that, there is something missing, a nuance that feels out of reach, a poetry to her nature that cannot be fathomed or deciphered easily. She slaps the face of social norms; she behaves in manners that are simultaneously empowered whilst judged as unwomanly by medieval audiences. Her wrath and anger at her shaming is tangible in the pages and songs of myth, her revenge is swift and unwavering. She crackles with stubbornness, with fury and resentment, she abandons her children to fates unknown – or at least they appear unknown on the surface of things. She teases reactions that are pitifully and obviously human, and she does so in a manner that invites the reader or the listener to 'feel' her presence – but who is she?

Humans have a peculiar relationship with story, they tug at heartstrings and evoke strong feelings and emotions, they can leave us feeling inspired, radiant, alive, or reeling with anger and disappointment. But story does so much more, it taps into a hidden depth of the fragile human mind and there accesses a wealth of wisdom just waiting to be put in accordance with the individual's virtues. The stories of Arianrhod are made the more complex by their origin in the Welsh language and cultural continuum of Wales. Subtle nuances can easily be lost in translation. Complexities of narration can be muddled in their interpretation, and mystery can easily descend into bewilderment.

For us to discover who Arianrhod is, we must descend into the cauldron of culture that served to preserve her memory and function to a people and a land that have long since been immersed in her story. For decades of pagan and polytheistic exploration, the details of Arianrhod have been expressed predominantly by non-Welsh speaking and reading individuals, who themselves were often reliant upon interpretation offered by non-native peoples. For the majority there was little choice, no option but to toe the line of familiarity and authority from previous authors and research. But today there is another way, a way through the beauty and subtle magic held in language and culture.

As a native Welsh person, the Arianrhod that I perceive, connect and work with as a divine being is the product of cultural immersion. She has been a continuous presence in my life since my childhood, the first stories told to me as an infant were those that contain her narrative. But what I must press upon you at this point is a peculiarity to the nature of the stories themselves. They were not presented as tales or stories that happened somewhere else, or once upon a time, but as elements of our culture that had an immanence, they were happening within that moment. This is profoundly transformative, for hearing these tales, myths and legends did not feel like passive entertainment, but rather akin to hearing news from home, a home that was just around the corner, one that the local bus would pass – if, of course, you had the courage to request a stop and delve into the dark forest of story. They were never far away or in a distant land, but instead were just out of sight, in your periphery, look with intention and they would appear. The tales did not happen 'Once upon a time', for the time of their telling is the time that they exist. The tales require one to literally become beside oneself and they would burst into technicolour life. I would gasp at the adventures of the characters of myth, but as I stepped into adulthood, I chose to intentionally step into their world fully, and in that stepping they became my gods, my magical allies and companions upon a path of pagan polytheism that would forever transform my life.

The myths became moments in my life. And as we progress through this book, I shall elaborate on what it truly means to experience a myth in the moment. The little details, which on the surface may sometimes appear superfluous or unnecessary are in the experience of a native-person necessary indeed. For the smallest of details can open a door onto a new landscape of deific exploration. In offering a native perspective, I offer you a way in which to see the goddess at hand through new eyes, those that are informed by centuries of influence from the rich cauldron of Welsh culture. In doing so, my aim is to transport you to the wonder I felt as a child that initiated a wandering into enchantment.

Is Arianrhod a goddess?

For the purposes of this book within the spectrum of contemporary western paganism, Arianrhod is presented as a goddess within the Welsh/Celtic Cultural Continuum. Whilst no evidence exists to suggest that Arianrhod was revered or worshipped in the past, no shrines or cults to her have ever been found, this does not negate her function as a deity in modern polytheism. By process of apotheosis, she has evolved to become a deity appropriate to modern polytheistic practises. Over the last two centuries or more, a plethora of archetypes and characters from Welsh myth have been elevated to the rank of deity, this is significant for it tells us something about the nature of culture and the needs of people. Whilst several Welsh mythological figures have cognates in the deep past and may well be echoes of an older pantheon, we do not need the permission of the past to authenticate an experience of the divine.

Arianrhod has become a valued and valid goddess for the new world and the new age, and several factors have gone into the making of this. Wales is steeped in magic and occult lore, and it is the opinion of this author that the spiritual principles behind these figures have also had a hand in the making of a god or goddess.

To return to that elusive question – who is she? The intention of this book is to present to you an exploration of the many aspects of Arianrhod, and how time and opinion has influenced her development. She is many things, and yet her fundamental virtues are unchanged. Over the past century, many have attempted to box her into one meaning: an almost impossible task. The following pages will explore those qualities that are fundamentally hers, and in doing so, reveal to you a goddess who is equally as deserving of praise and honour as any other deity in modern polytheistic practices. There is perhaps a reason why Arianrhod is not as popular as Cerridwen, as Brigid or the Morrigan – it lies in her complexity and the way in which she has been misunderstood. But she waits for you nonetheless, to find your way to her – and in that finding you will be transformed.

My aim in this short tome is to introduce you to aspects of Arianrhod that you may not have considered, not to change your relationship entirely, but to offer you windows of inspiration and wisdom that will transform the nature of that relationship. To deepen your understanding of who and what she is, and how her virtues can be emulated in your life. Surely, this is the aim and purpose of any polytheistic act of connection and devotion. To emulate and mirror the virtues of the gods in our own lives and living, to express those virtues into the wider world. To inspire our square miles and contribute to a river of inspiration that was old when this world was at its newest.

How to use this book

Read the book sequentially from beginning to end before attempting any of the practises offered to you at its conclusion. The aim of the practises are to deepen your connection to the goddess, but it is imperative that you first 'get to know her'. That is a function of this book, to provide you with a window onto a mythic landscape that contains the essence of a powerful deity. Deific relationships are not one-way streets, the most effective and profound are symbiotic, where the deity and devotee are equally enriched by the experience. In essence the explorative components of this book are essentially an opportunity for you to date the divine, and to discover a personality that underlies the many assumptions made about her.

Each chapter begins with a poem, these are invocatory in nature and their positions in this book are entirely intentional. They too can be used by yourself as invocations of praise, devotion and connection. Read each one aloud prior to reading the chapter.

Whilst this is primarily a book about Arianrhod, she does not exist in a vacuum, she is part of a mythical landscape replete with complex relationship. At times it is necessary for the nature of those relationships and the characters that interact with Arianrhod to be examined in relation to her. She is coloured by the quality of the relationships she has with the other inhabitants of myth, just as you are influenced and painted by the various relationships in your life.

Whilst relatively short in terms of words, this book is intended to be a journey of devotion and praise from me to you in honour of the goddess that I love. This is a love affair that is joyfully expressed in the hope that you too will fall in love with the goddess in a similar manner to my experience, and in doing so be transformed by the depth and quality of that relationship.

So, come with me on a journey to the island of Arianrhod and there to gaze at her radiance and be bestowed by her grace, beauty, dignity and power.

Chapter one

What's in a Name?

Arianrhod, goddess of the silver wheel,
Mystery and wisdom in your name concealed,
You weave the threads of fate with skill,
To your child, your destiny now distil.

Radiant dawn and raging river,
Your mystery held in gold and silver,
You hold the key to my destiny,
My journey through life's tapestry.

A still point on the wheel of time,
Aranrhod, your wisdom is spoke in rhyme,
Fates now woven and spun by your hand,
Guiding my spirit to understand.

Oh Arianrhod, mother of rebirth,
In your raging wisdom, I find my worth,
Bless me with your grace divine,
As I walk the path of your design.

There is an elephant in the room, and one that needs addressing before we can commence with the remainder of this book – what is the name of this goddess? A quick internet search will reveal that there are two distinct versions of her name – Arianrhod and Aranrhod. But why the difference? This is a complex issue that needs careful dissection, but in doing so we run the risk of damaging the internal organs that bring life to each name in turn, for both are valid and worthy; therefore, my evisceration of each term must proceed cautiously.

In my own practise I do not refer to her as Arianrhod but rather I know her as Aranrhod, this is not to suggest that one is correct and the other not. It is a complicated issue that has been exacerbated by centuries of influence and inspiration. The key to that first sentence is in my deliberate use of the term 'I know her', for my choice of name expresses the nature of the relationship I have with Aranrhod. Do not fear or despond, for there is good reason for this and in exploring the spelling of her name in both cases, we can discern much about the nature of the goddess.

In Welsh culture names are powerful things, not only do they act as identifiers, but they contain within them hidden aspects that refer to the nature of something. In Welsh mythology many of the names are not simply personal nouns, but sometimes adjectives and verbs. They have an uncanny ability to refer to a person or personage as an aspect of the human condition. This is relevant to the name Arianrhod/Aranrhod, the name itself is trying to tell you something by bestowing a deeper level of meaning to the energy, archetype, spirit or deity that it is representing. In other words, the name of deity contains a truth that reflects their inherent attributes and virtues. In fact, one of the first places we should look when dealing with the Welsh gods is to their names.

By exploring the nature of her name within this first chapter, your perception of her will be forever altered, and a new perspective and wisdom will be achieved by proxy. From a magical perspective this is akin to the goddess reaching out from the moment of myth to impact upon you – right here and now.

These moments of clarity and inspiration are significant and important in that they express a connection in the now. She is not located somewhere else, she is not situated in a distant time, there is no once-upon-a-time. The time is now, and she is immanent and imminent. The immanence of this exploration is the positioning of the goddess within the moment, the imminency of it is her arrival in your consciousness. Whenever you feel a sense of clarity, or a moment of 'gosh, I didn't know that!', mark those instances as occasions in which the goddess is reaching out to you. Your sense of her, and her sense of you are held magically within those moments.

To the ancient Druids of the British Isles, the memory of which are held in the myths that speak of Arianrhod, words were magical talismans and the writing of them were forbidden, perhaps for fear of unleashing their power. In that spirit, these words act in the same manner, each word in her praise and honour are doorways onto her landscape. Your task is to decide whether to step through or not. But I press upon you the significance of magical mythic moments in which you feel or sense a transformation in your relationship with her, or a deepening of understanding. Take note, take heed and proceed acknowledging that she is indeed present within this moment.

A Designation Dissection

When considering the nature of her name, our first reference is from medieval times and in the body of work known as *The Mabinogion*; a collection of 11 Welsh myths that record the lives and adventures of characters which have become deities of modern polytheistic movements. Within this collection is a sub-category of myths called 'The Four Branches of the Mabinogi', each one is intimately connected to the other, like the intricate weaving of Celtic knotwork. We shall explore the specifics of these myths later in relation to Arianrhod. In her translation with an introduction and notes, Welsh scholar Sioned Davies consistently uses the name Aranrhod. The first reference to her in this work is as *'Aranrhod daughter of Dôn'*[1], Davies then uses the spelling Aranrhod consistently throughout the text. However, in her notes she refers to the other form of her name –

> *"In the Triads (TYP 35), [Aranrhod] she is the daughter of Beli son of Mynogan. Her name sometimes occurs as Arianrhod."*[2]

In the Welsh language version of the same body of myth – *Y Mabinogion* by Dafydd and Rhiannon Ifans, they choose to use the spelling Arianrhod, implying that there is a general acceptance within Welsh culture that this spelling is also correct. Unfortunately, and unlike Davies they do not offer a rationale or reason for choosing that spelling.[3]

Mark Williams in his *'The Celtic Myths that shape the way we think'*, and his exploration of the same body of myth elects to use the spelling 'Aranrhod' consistently.[4] American academic, Patrick K. Ford in his work on the Fourth Branch of the Mabinogi collection maintains this position by claiming –

> *"The evidence seems to favour the form Aranrot…"*[5]

In contrast the name that appears in the body of work called *'Trioedd Ynys Prydein'* (the Triads of the Island of Britain), a collection of lore and allegory recorded in a tripartite fashion, appears with a slightly different spelling *'Aryanrot'.*[6] She is mentioned three times in the triads, twice with the spelling 'Aryanrot' and once as the more common 'Aranrot'. The editor of the work – Rachel Bromwich notes that –

> *"Aranrot appears consistently throughout the Fourth Branch of the Mabinogi in the texts of the White Book of Rhydderch and the Red Book of Hergest. But Aryanrot is the spelling of the name in triad number 35."*[7]

She concluded that –

> *"…and the evidence of the Book of Taliesin 36.15 combined with that of the spelling Aranrot, which is uniform throughout*

> *the Mabinogi, strongly favours Aranrot as the original form, as against Aryanrot."*[8]

The work that Bromwich is referring to as the *Book of Taliesin* is a collection of medieval Welsh poetry attributed to the semi-historical but mostly legendary chief Bard of Welsh culture – Taliesin, meaning 'radiant or shining brow'. Further references to this figure will be elaborated upon in connection with Arianrhod later in this work.

But why the differences? What light can the two different spellings offer the polytheist in their attempt to deepen their connection to the goddess?

Aranrot? Aranrhod? Aryanrot? Arianrhod?

The names have different meanings, but to dive into them and glean any wisdom we are required to investigate the past. One source of note to the quandary of her name, and which has been unavailable to non-Welsh audiences is a body of work by the late Sir Ifor Williams. He was an eminent Welsh scholar who dedicated his professional career to the study and advancement of Welsh literature. His *'Pedeir Keinc y Mabinogi – allan o Lyfr Gwyn Rhydderch'* (Four Branches of the Mabinogi from the *White Book of Rhydderch*) offers an extensive introduction, text and notes to the Four Branches in their entirety. It is within his notes pertaining to the Fourth Branch that contains the myth in which Arianrhod appears that we must look. I include the original Welsh below and for the first time in the English language, a translation –

> *"Aranrot, anodd dweud beth yw elfennau'r enw, Aran ai ynteu Arian; rhod ai ynteu rhawd. Tuedda Gruffydd i'w gydio wrth hen enw Strassburg, sef Argentoratum neu Argentorate, gan gymryd bod 'rat' – yn cynnwys 'a' hir. Os felly Arian, a rhawd fel yn bedd – rawd. Rhaid tybio mai engraifft gynnar sydd*

yma o droi '-aw' yn 'o' yn y sillaf olaf, os derbynnir hyn. Yn erbyn hynny, y mae absenoldeb enghraifft o'r ffurf Arianrawd yn unman; ond profir '-rot' gan yr odl cyn gynhared, beth bynnag, ag oedd y gân yn B.T, 36, 'aranrot drem clot'. Hyd yn oed pe delid mai ffugiant yw'r gân, er hynny dengys mai '-rot' oedd y terfyniad yr enw i'r ffugiwr: ni chlywsai ac ni welsai – 'rawt' ynddo yn yr hengerdd.

Anos yw yr elfen gyntaf: 'silver wheel' medd Rhys, H.L 284, ac yn wir ceir amryw enwau'n cynnwys arian yn ddiamheuol; fel hen enwau Llydewig, Argant-hael, argant-louuen etc, ac hefyd am enw merch mewn hen Gymraeg, Arganhell, cf, Ariannell, yn bentref Ariannell ym Môn... Yn R.M 298, rhoir y tri 'aryanllu'; "ar trydydd a aeth gan gaswallawn fab Beli, a Gwennwynwyn a Gwanar feibion Lliaws Fab Nwyfre ac Aryanrot ferch Veli eu mam". Ymhobman arall yn R.M. ceir 'aranrot'. Rhaid felly, ystyried y posibilrwydd mai aran yw'r elfen gyntaf, ac nad yw Arianrod ond ffrwyth cydweddiad. Yn y cyswllt hwn ystyrier yr enwau a rydd Holder, megis Arandis, Aranni, Arani, Arandunum, Arania, Aranto etc. Hefyd enwau'r mynyddoedd, Yr Aran, Yr Aran Fawr, Aran Benllyn, a'r bychanigyn Arennig. Ni cholli'r 'I' gytsain yn Arfon a Meirionydd, a phrofa'r rhain y ffurf Aran, neu Garan."[9]

Translation –

"*Aranrot*, it is hard to tell what the elements of the name are, *Aran* or *Arian*; *Rhod* or *Rhawd*. Gruffydd tends to take it from Strasbourg's old name, which is *Argentoratum* or *Argentorate*, assuming that *rat* – contains a long â. If it is *Arian*, and *rhawd* as in beddrawd meaning grave mound. I should assume that this is an early example of turning *-aw* into *o* in the last syllable, if this can be accepted. Against that, there is the absence of an example of the *Arianrawd* form anywhere; but *-rot* is proved by the rhyme of early works, in any case, with the song in the *Book of Taliesin,* 36, *aranrot drem clot.* Even if it were held that the song is a fiction, nevertheless it shows that the ending of the name for the scribe was *-rot*: he would not have heard and would not have seen *-rawt* in the old poems.

The first element is more difficult: *silver wheel* says Rhys, H.L (Lectures on Celtic Heathendom) 284, and indeed there are several names that undoubtedly contain *arian;* such as old Breton names, *Argant-hael, argant-louuen* etc (the g is pronounced as a soft e sound), and also for a girl's name in old Welsh, *Arganhell, Ariannell,* and the village of *Ariannell* in Anglesey. In The text of the Mabinogion from the *Red Book of Hergest,* Rhys-Evans (R.M), 298 draws attention to the three silvers (*aryanallu*) that are given; *"and the third went with Caswallawn the son of Beli, and Gwennwynwyn and Gwanar the sons of Lliaws the Son of Nwyfre and Aryanrot the daughter of Beli, their mother".* Everywhere else in R.M. it is consistently *aranrot.* We must therefore consider the possibility that *aran* is the first element, and that *Arianrod* is only the fruit of concordance. In this connection consider the names of the mountains, *Yr Aran, Yr Aran Fawr, Aran Benllyn,* and the diminutive *Arennig.* A consonant is not lost in Arfon and Meirionydd, and these prove the form Aran, is derived from Garan."[10]

There is a lot to unpack here, but in its unpacking, we glean some of the mystery that is hidden within her name. For clarification, an explanation is required as to the different letters used in the construction of the consistent – Aranrot. For the modern mind the terminal letter 't' is simply that, appearing as it would in English and carrying a 't' sound as in 'tea'. However, in Middle

Welsh the letter 't' following a vowel is pronounced as a soft 'd' sound, as in 'dinner'. A further complexity can be seen in more recent centuries where the name as exemplified terminates with the suffix *'rhod'* as opposed to the manuscript spelling 'rod'. This may all seem rather over-complicated, but there are subtle details here that are important in understanding how her name is constructed and what it may have sounded like in antiquity. When we consider that the scribes are trying their best to record sounds, some of which may be alien to them, the discrepancy in spelling makes sense.

It is likely that the consistent spelling of her name – Aranrot evolved into 'Aranrhod' in scholarly and academic works of the past century or so. This evolution of the name is interesting for it offers us an opportunity to hear her name clearly as it was heard by Welsh ears. This sound is utterly absent when non-Welsh eyes are attempting to discern the sound of a word from letters on parchment alone.

For the non-Welsh mind, the terminus 'rod' may be pronounced exactly as it appears on paper, as in 'fishing rod'. However, the 'rh' sound is not found in English, it is a rolling 'r' sound with a combined audible exhalation verging on the 'h' sound in 'huff'. It is quite difficult to replicate for non-Welsh speaking tongues. Consequently, the English pronunciation of both Aranrhod and the common Arianrhod tend to be ARRAN-rod, or arr-ee-ANN-rod. In her native language, her name would be accurately pronounced in both instances as 'ARRAN-rhod', or 'arr-ee-ANN-rhod', note that the emphasis of any word in Welsh is on the penultimate syllable.

Pronunciation aside for a moment, what can these syllables mean, do they represent actual words and what wisdom can we glean? Let's begin by examining the terminal syllable of her name as it appears in its most consistent form within the manuscripts – Aranrot.

The Silver Wheel

To consult the University of Wales's dictionary of the Welsh language we will discover that the suffix *'rot'* is directly related to the Indo European *'rot'* meaning wheel, which gave rise to the Latin term *'rota'*, also meaning wheel.[11] The meaning and significance of *rot* or *rhod* in modern Welsh is *olwyn* which literally and figuratively means wheel. It also signifies a sphere or a circle, the orbit of a planet, the firmament or heavens, and refers to fortune and perhaps most interestingly – fate. These correlations are present in the common neo-pagan meaning of the name Arianrhod as 'the Silver Wheel'. Whilst the silver element is problematic for some scholars, and a matter we will deal with presently, it can safely be said that the suffix *rhod* does refer to something that is turning, spinning or in perpetual motion, or indeed related to fate. When we consider the mythological function and attributes of Arianrhod's as a goddess figure who is responsible for the doling out of fate, this adds an interesting and relevant feature to her name. So, now we are getting closer to understanding the mechanism of her name and what it may tell us about her nature.

In studying her name, we must consider the meanings of both Aran and Arian to understand the dynamics of meaning, for both have an important part to play in the making of the goddess. We will begin by considering the nature of the common form of her name in the 21st century as – Arianrhod and delve into the prefix -Arian. In accordance with the popular translation of her name as 'silver wheel', this would on the surface appear to be quite correct. By consulting the *Geiriadur Prifysgol Cymru* (The Dictionary of the Welsh Language) it can be determined that the term *'arian'* refers to the metal silver, the chemical element, or to anything that shines with a silvery and bright light (*llwydwyn* in Welsh). Literally it is also a term for money and currency, in particular coins, owing in all probability to the silvery appearance of the common Iron Age copper alloy and potin coins. Potin is a tin-rich copper-alloy and gave the coins a distinctive bright grey appearance. Figuratively arian is used to describe the beauty of melodious sounds that are pleasing to the ear, in particular sounds created by voice or birdsong.

The origin of arian is the Indo-European term *ə̥rĝn̥to-*, from the original *arĝ* meaning something that appeared as white or had a distinctive shine. It developed and evolved into the old, middle and modern dialects of Celtic languages suggesting that there was an understanding of the term across different Celtic cultures with differing language structures, with each culture using the term to define something as being silver or bright grey in appearance or nature. In Old Cornish it frequently appears as a personal noun in the form of *argan* (with the 'g' sound being pronounced as an 'ee'), in Middle Cornish it is found as *ar(g) hans*. Old and Middle Breton record the term as *'argant'* and *'archant'* respectively. In Old Irish it can be found as *'argat'*, to mean silver. The Gaulish tongue often used the term in describing places and personal nouns with one example being *'Arganto'* as a term meaning 'magus'. The same term is seen in Celtiberia as *'arkato'*. Each of these would have evolved from the proto-Celtic term *'arganto'*. These can be compared to the Latin term *'argentum'* meaning silver.

Whilst each branch of the differing Celtic tongues is unique and expressive of individual cultures, there is a commonality at the foundation of those languages that implies an inherent, ancestral connection. The various terms for silver in each language is demonstrative of this. In his notes Williams provides examples of the many instances in Celtic culture where the term arian is used in various dialects to describe locations and given as a typical female name. This gives some credence to the term arian being used as a prefix for the name in question, particularly when we consider that the scribes of the Triads of Britain chose that designation rather than the more consistent aran. Their motivations have been obscured by time, but scholars have offered some hypothetical suggestions over the past century, with Williams concluding that it is likely the 'fruit of concordance'. If the name Arianrhod is indeed the product of concordance, as polytheists we can maybe accept that the goddess herself had a hand in the making of her new name, one applicable for a new audience in a new age.

In considering her silvery attributes we must also address the modern associations and attributes placed upon Arianrhod. In contemporary pagan practise she has evolved to be a goddess of the moon, a star goddess, associated with the Corona Borealis or the Northern Crown. She is often identified as a goddess of reincarnation, fate and destiny but also with divination, prophesy and the dead. Robert Graves in his *White Goddess* claimed that she is another aspect of Cerridwen and a goddess who rules a state of purgatory in her magical fort.[12] Whilst none of these attributes are particularly problematic, they do convey a tendency of causing something to fit with an agenda or a remit. This is not to point a finger of blame, her mysteries have been locked into language and culture for centuries, and often new ideas are developed from outdated or incorrect conclusions. What this book serves to achieve is to provide a native perspective that reveals mysteries that were otherwise fettered by culture.

Her association with the moon as the silver wheel whilst it may be symbolically obvious, it is tenuous at best. The Corona Borealis is identified as Caer Arianrhod in Welsh literature, but this seemingly is from the pen and imagination of the poetic genius and literal forger – Iolo Morganwg. There is little evidence beyond him to substantiate a claim that Arianrhod is connected to the constellation. Others have made a comparison between the physical location of the fort, off the coast of northwest Wales, and the position of the Corona Borealis in proximity to the Milky Way.[13] These ideas are intriguing and beautiful, but alas, they have little foundation within the mythical and Bardic traditions of Wales. What they demonstrate is the desire and need for people to make associations with something that they feel is important to them.

Putting the silvery component aside for now, we turn our attention towards the earlier consistent form of her name – Aranrot and consider the prefix *'aran'*.

Mountains and Still Points

In his notes, Williams tended to favour the prefix aran as opposed to arian and refers to the various mountains in North Wales that contain it as a component of their names. Interestingly the mountains he refers to are in the region that Arianrhod's primary mythology is located. In his observation Williams briefly touches upon a peculiarity of the Welsh language, mutations, in which significant meaning can be gleaned but paradoxically made unavailable to those who do not comprehend them.

In almost every instance of aran in the northwest counties of Arfon and Meirionydd that border the lands of Arianrhod and her immediate family group, the term follows a definite article, *y* or *yr (the)*. This causes a soft mutation of the first vowel of a proceeding noun, and we can clearly see that at work in the examples offered by Williams – Yr Aran, Yr Aran Fawr, and implied in the spelling of the mountains Aran Benllyn and Arennig. Williams believed that the same principle applied to Aranrhod, in that the original form of her name possibly contained a definite article and forces the subsequent noun to change its form and sound.

On the other hand, Celtic academic Rachel Bromwich suggested another possible meaning in that aran could be a reference to something that is huge, round or humped.[14]. Hypothetically this may be a reference to the appearance of Arianrhod's fort, which appears from the seas in the Caernarfon area of northwest Wales as a series of rocks upon a low mound or hump.

However, this may be quite a stretch and I am inclined to lean towards Williams' theory of mutational change which makes more sense from a Welsh perspective, in which case *aran* appears as the mutation of *garan*. Mutational rules affect the initial letter of a word depending on the context, in this case the consonant 'g' is subject to a soft mutation when preceded by the definite article. When subjected to this form of mutation the 'g' sound disappears entirely, leaving the next letter as the starting point of the word at hand, in this case it would be rendered as the letter and sound 'a'.

According to the *Dictionary of the Welsh Language* the term garan has two distinct meanings, the first being a crane or a heron and the second referring to a leg, shaft, shank or axle. Context is required to determine which meaning is used in a particular word. For example, in the folktale of Cerridwen the Witch goddess of inspiration, and a poem attributed to the legendary poet – Taliesin, a figure by the name of Gwyddno Garanhir is referred to. Gwyddno is likely to mean something relating to trees or a specific tree relevant to his nature or family line. You will note that the designation 'garan' is given to this individual as the prefix of his surname or second name. In this case the suffix 'hir' meaning long or tall, tells us that garan is used to mean leg or shank rather than axle or shaft, but might also mean crane. As a result, the common translation of the surname Garanhir is – Long-legs, Long-Shanks, Crane-legs or literally the 'Tall-crane'. All of this might be an indication that this figure was particularly tall or had distinguishable legs. When we consider the name Aranrhod, it is evident from the structure of the word and its suffix meaning wheel or something that is turning that we are unlikely to be dealing with a reference to her legs or shanks; but rather to the more mysterious, and perhaps on immediate appearance, the nonsensical – axle, or shaft.

Whilst initially perplexing, the Welsh language tends to hide and reveal mystery in intriguing manners, some of which are not always obvious to the untrained eye. To find meaning we must examine the nature of an axle and how that might assist us in interpreting her name. The function of an axle is a shaft or rod inserted into the central point of two wheels thus allowing for their smooth turning. But how does this relate to the function of Aranrhod? To dig deeper into this, we need to expand our view briefly and consider cognate themes in other cultures.

The Sacred Axle

The function of an axle in spirituality is not uncommon. If we look to Hindu and Buddhist sources the necessity for a stable axle is essential for the turning of the wheels of life. The *Dharmachakra* or the Wheel of Dharma is an important symbol of three parts, a hub, spokes and a rim, with each part expressing significance and the teachings of Buddhism, Hinduism and Jainism. If the wheel becomes unstable it can lead to a state of *Duhkha,* commonly referred to as a state of suffering because of an unbalanced or misplaced axle. If the axle is incorrectly positioned, the wheels of life are likely to become unbalanced. Duhkha forms part of the three marks of existence and appears in Hindu scriptures in discussions of Moksha or the state of spiritual liberation from the cycles of life, death and rebirth. The state of *Sukha,* or happiness implies that the axle has been correctly positioned resulting in the smooth turning of the wheels of life.

The wheel and its axle or axis as a metaphor can be seen as a prominent symbol in other world religions and spiritualties from Christianity to Native American Culture. Whilst these cultures differ on many levels, the symbol of the wheel carries a universality in that it represents fundamental aspects of the human condition and spirituality, and is used a symbol of movement and progression, and the pursuit of spiritual illumination. It is associated with the cycles of life, death and rebirth to this day, in modern Pagan practise the Wheel of the Year has become synonymous with the mysteries and cycles of life, death, rebirth and rejuvenation. The axle is essential for the proper equilibrium of wheels and provides the driving force to propel them forwards in a balanced fashion. In doing so, the axle maintains a force that keeps the wheels spinning in relation to one another, even if the wheels are a distance apart.

In the English language the older term for axle was axletree, a term that is still used in some engineering circles, particularly in relation to motorised vehicles. I find this term particularly interesting in that a tree is used in relation to a mechanism that forms a still and balanced point at the centre of a structure, and it is tempting to make analogies with the ancient, cross-cultural references to the Axis Mundi, or World Tree, a visionary concept where a tree holds the spinning parts of all existence in perfect harmony – just like an axle. An axis is essentially a real or an imaginary line that runs through the centre of an object, in turn an axle runs along an axis.

The Stillness at the Centre

Taken from this perspective, the name Aranrhod can be interpreted as the still point, the centre, the facilitator of turning wheels. The implication here is that Aranrhod is not the wheel per-se, but rather the force that enables its turning. When we consider this in relation to her actions in her primary mythology – the Fourth Branch of the Mabinogi – our perspective of her function can change dramatically. For hidden within her name is a quality that expresses the action of someone who knew exactly what she was doing. She is often misunderstood and judged for her actions in her myth. However, when we consider the meaning of her name, a mystery is made clearer. As an axle, her function is the turning of not one, but two wheels, linked together by her power and momentum. The subjects that the wheels represent may not be conscious of each other, but they are turning in relation to the force that she imposes. She is the axle that drives the wheels of the entire myth towards the ultimate transformation/initiation of the main protagonist, we shall delve deeper into this later. In the narrative she is often portrayed and can appear as the obvious antagonist, and this would have been highly entertaining for a Medieval audience, and yet when we scratch at the surface her secrets can be revealed.

With all this in mind, the function of Aranrhod has deepened, she is no longer just representative of a silver-wheel, which may be vague at best, but indicative of a force that underlies the actions held within her story. It is these details that are missing in modern translations, the nuance is lost, and hence modern polytheists can miss out on a hoard of deep meaning that is just waiting to be discovered.

If she is the axle that moves the wheels of mythology, we must also consider the mystery that myth is something that never happened, and yet they happen all the time, they are happening to you right now. When myth exists in the moment, we can perceive how the forces that Aranrhod governs are at play in your life this very second. When we move into this understanding, we can deepen our relationship with Aranrhod and her functionality. When we need to analyse the movement of the wheels of our living, the goddess that we should look to for advice and clarity is Aranrhod – the sacred axle, the axis around which your life turns.

As we progress through this book, I would like for you to keep the mysteries of the axle in mind. There are two wheels in operation here, on one side is me as the author of this work, and on the other is you, the reader. Between these two forces is the goddess, the axle herself, causing these wheels to spin along a particular axis and to follow the course of a specific trajectory – to understand and deepen relationship. Therefore, keep this mystery in mind, that at the centre of this work and of your exploration and discovery of Arianrhod, that she is a constant force, always at play, always intriguing and often surprising. When we keep the deity in mind in such a manner, it causes them to be simultaneously immanent and imminent. Her immanency is within this work, and within your budding relationship with her; her imminency is in her constant arriving and influence within each moment of the journey.

The Triads of the Island of Britain

Earlier in this chapter I briefly touched upon references to Arianrhod within a body of literature called 'Trioedd Ynys Pyrdain – The Triads of the Island of Britain.' In all likelihood, it is this collection of tripartite Bardic wisdoms that is responsible for the arian designation in Arianrhod.

Three triads record her name and further details that differ from the Fourth Branch of the Mabinogi. Triad number 35 says –

> *"The three levies that departed from this island, and not one of them came back:*
>
> *The first went with Elen of the Hosts and Cynan her brother, the second went with Yrp of the Hosts.*
>
> *The third levy went with Caswallawn son of Beli and Gwenwynwyn and Gwanar, sons of Lliaws the son of Nwyfre and Aryanrot daughter of Beli their mother...And those were the Three Silver Hosts."*[15]

Several details differ in this triad from her primary myth. The first is that her name is spelled 'Aryanrot', in the original Middle

Welsh, and rendered as Arianrhod in the text and translation by Rachel Bromwich. One hypothesis for this inconsistent spelling might be the responsibility of the redactor who was attempting to connect the Aryan component of Aryanrot with the Welsh term for the Three Silver Hosts – Y Tri Aryanllu. However, Bromwich suggested that owing to the consistent form of her name being Aranrot in the manuscripts there is a possibility that the Tri Aryanallu is itself an error and that its original form might have been – aranllu.[16]

In stark contrast to the independent woman that we find occupying the mythical landscape of the Fourth Branch. The Arianrhod of the Triads is markedly different, the mythical Aranrhod has no obligations to a man, and actively denounces motherhood. In Triad 35 she is the consort of a man called Lliaws Fab Nwyfre and the mother of two boys, Gwenwynwyn and Gwanar. Additionally, in the Mabinogi she is identified as the daughter of Dôn, who is generally accepted as a parent deity or mother goddess in modern polytheism. In the Triads she is identified as the daughter of Beli, an ancestor deity that many Welsh dynasties claimed to be descended from. The triads portray a figure that is almost the opposite of the one we find in the Fourth Branch of the Mabinogi.

In her myth she is the daughter of an earthy figure, Dôn who is cognate with the Irish Danu. She appears as an over-mother, or a great mother goddess whose mythology has been subsequently lost. In contemporary polytheism Dôn is associated with rivers and the land. In contrast Beli is more often associated with the sky owing to his over-arching influence and how he connects different tribes and dynasties. This sky or airy component is emulated in the consort of Arianrhod – Lliaws fab Nwyfre whose name literally means – Host, multitude son of sky/atmosphere. Whilst this name does appear in obscure manuscripts, it is unclear what his role was, and he may be indicative of a lost body of lore. Their offspring, however, pose an interesting quandary, Gwenwynwyn whose name translates to – Shining Bright Poison or Killer, this peculiar name is found only in a Mid Welsh ruler in the 13th Century, nothing else is known of this character. Likewise, his brother Gwanar, whose name translates as – Warrior Lord, is also unknown in the native tales and myths.

Whilst this Triad offers little in the form of illumination it does provide a source for the spelling Arianrhod. The remaining Triads, however, return us to the familiar territory of Arianrhod's mythology.

Triad 67 says –

> *"Three golden shoemakers of the Island of Britain:*
> *Caswallon son of Beli...and Manawydan son of Llŷr, and Lleu Llaw Gyffes, when he and Gwydion were seeking a name and arms from his mother Aranrhod (Aranrot in the original manuscript)."*[17]

Note the return to the consistent spelling of Aranrhod and the continuity of themes from the Fourth Branch of the Mabinogi.

Triad number 78 revisits the Aryanrot spelling –

> *"The three fair and royal ladies of the Island of Britain:*
> *Creirwy, daughter of Ceridwen, and Arianrhod daughter of Dôn, and Gwen daughter of Cywryd son of Crydon."*[18]

Whilst the redactor chooses Arianrhod, the triad confirms the mythical sources that identifies Arianrhod as the daughter of Dôn.

Later references in poetry from the 15th century onwards tend to lean towards the Arianrhod spelling, whilst the storytelling tradition seemingly preferred the designation Aranrhod.

Finding Meaning

To conclude this examination of Arianrhod vs Aranrhod, what is the meaning of her name? As this discourse has demonstrated, she is as complex and colourful as the language that preserved her memory. She is simultaneously the lady of the silver wheel in modern paganism, she is the wheel of fate and the turning of celestial bodies, she is the still point at the centre, the force and power that turns the wheels of life and existence. She can be all those things, all at once, or some of those things at certain times. However, our understanding of her does not conclude with an exploration of her name, it is merely the first diving board, there is a depth of wonder ahead. As we progress on this journey in search of her, even more details will come to light that will add further ingredients of understanding into the cauldron of relationship.

These details are of interest to those seeking to deepen their understanding of how a deity evolves and develops through time, but we may consider that other forces are also at play. Arianrhod is a goddess that holds significance and meaning to a host of individuals in modern polytheism, and it is not the intention of this book to denigrate that connection, or to insist that she be called by her earlier consistent form of Aranrot in Middle Welsh, and Aranrhod in Modern Welsh, or Arianrhod. I believe that she can be called by either designation albeit the meanings may differ – for myself, I consider that Aranrhod is the Modern Welsh designation, whilst Arianrhod is that which has become meaningful for a non-Welsh speaking demographic. Ultimately the name one chooses to use distils to the principle of relationship and the quality and depth of that relationship. From an occult perspective I have long suggested that eager devotees ask the goddess by which designation she wishes you to refer to her, in the same manner that in modern times it is polite to ask an individual which pronoun they prefer, it is perhaps equally as courteous to enquire of the goddess herself.

The Welsh language is ancient and complex and can express mystery and intrigue with surprising results, but sometimes, a native voice is required to tease these mysteries out of the hidden realms and into awareness. Language carries culture, and cultural references can be locked and remain inaccessible to those outside of said culture. It is the task of someone like me to bring these details out of secrecy and into a framework that will deepen your understanding and heighten the quality of your relationship with deity.

Now that we have taken a deep dive into the nature of her name, it is time to continue our journey and look to the mythic and other sources that preserve her story and memory. From this point forward, you will note that I will use the spellings Aranrhod and Arianrhod interchangeably, at times it will appear obvious why I choose a certain version, at other times my motivations may not be as apparent. To reiterate my earlier claim, neither is more correct than the other, both contain mystery and meaning and are equally relevant.

Chapter 2

Spinning the Wheel of Myth

Arianrhod, mysterious and wise,
Goddess of fate before my eyes.
Spin now the wheel, weave destiny's thread,
From your island realm your truth is shared.

Between the realms, composed and still,
Weaver of fates, bestower of will.
Daughter of sky, and sister of sea,
Mistress of land, I beckon thee.

When seeking the nature of deity there are various resources at our disposal. Modern polytheistic and pagan writers have contributed an immense amount to our understanding of deity over the past several decades, but it is also important that we look to source materials that reflect the culture from which the deity emerges and is preserved. It is pertinent at this juncture to glean information from the sources that carry the spirit of Arianrhod through time, and who those people may have been, and what wisdom we can access from the ancestral material they left.

To achieve this, I shall list the primary sources in which we find references to the goddess. I shall offer a brief description of the material and then commence to dive deeper into them over the coming pages and chapters.

Aranrhod is specifically Welsh in nature, the material that pertains to her comes exclusively from Welsh culture. Whilst there may be similarities between her name and European place names, there is little beyond the boundaries of Wales that refer to a character as unique and perplexing as Aranrhod.

The primary sources for Arianrhod/Aranrhod are –

- The *White Book of Rhydderch* – containing the Four Branches of the Mabinogi
- The *Red Book of Hergest* – containing a version of the Four Branches of the Mabinogi
- The Triads of the Islands of Britain
- The *Book of Taliesin*
- Peniarth Manuscript 131 & Llansteffan Manuscript 28[19]
- Gwaith Lewys Môn
- Ystoria Taliesin: National Library of Wales Manuscript 5276D
- Hanes Taliesin: Peniarth Manuscript 111

Whilst several primary sources are available and offer intriguing insights into the nature of Arianrhod, it is perhaps the Fourth Branch of the Mabinogi that is most famed for her story. This is the magic of storytelling and narrative that reaches the present from ancient times, carrying the spirit of Arianrhod to the here and now. To glean wisdom, it is pertinent that we look to the mechanisms that served to preserve her and their significance to Welsh culture past and present.

The Magic of the Bard & Storyteller

Welsh culture is steeped in the power of the spoken word, but to make this statement is not to hearken back to an idealistic past populated by Bards on every street corner, but rather to ascertain that we continue to be a Bardic and poetic culture to this day. The Welsh Bardic Tradition is a system of Bardic teaching and practise that has its roots in the deep past and its branches in the modern world. Welsh culture does not commend its citizens for financial prowess or fetes of war and politics, but instead the highest accolade our culture bestows is upon the Bard who can produce the best poem. Each year, three bards are chosen to be awarded the Bardic chair, the crown or blue-ribbon medal in recognition of their abilities by the Gorsedd of Bards of the Island of Britain at Wales's largest cultural festival – the National Eisteddfod. There is something deeply humbling and beautiful about a culture that places its utmost respect and recognition upon the creation of poetry.

The living branches of Bardism in Wales, and its echoes of ancient spirits and what we now identify as gods and goddesses make frequent reference to the characters that inhabit the world of myth. The fact that so many of these poems' pre-date the written versions of the Mabinogi hint at their ancient roots. Welsh culture consisted of two specialised disciplines that are pertinent to this discourse, the Bard and the Storyteller, but to understand their mechanics we must unpack them a little.

Essentially the Bard was the keeper of culture and the wisdom inherent within it. The etymological root of Bard has its foundation in Old Celtic in the form of *'bardos'*, meaning a poet or singer. In turn 'bardos' has its roots in Proto Indo-European *'gwredho'* meaning 'he who makes praises'. It is a term that is simultaneously ancient and modern and of cultural significance in Wales.[20] In the Welsh language the term for Bard is *'Bardd'*, with the 'dd' terminus pronounced in the exact manner as the 'th' sound in 'them'. Its roots reach back into the last golden age of the British Celts of two thousand years ago, by the time the term was being written on parchment between the 7th and 9th centuries it was already well over a thousand years old.

Not only were the Bards preservers of culture, but they also had access to a storehouse of cultural knowledge preserved in the guise of 'triads'; wisdoms set out in a tripartite structure for ease of memory. The earliest references to Arianrhod stems from this period. The Bards did not express simple poetry, albeit its apparent ornamentation was and is significant, they simultaneously conveyed a deeper meaning, or an *'ystyr hud'* in

Welsh, or what Dr. Gwilym Morus-Baird refers to as symbolic meaning that expresses a deeper mystery accessed by metaphor and symbols.[21] The Bardic tradition is a system that has metaphysical attributions woven into the fabric of the words themselves, it is an expression of magic.[22]

The prototypic and mystical Bard – Taliesin – intimately connected to the tale of Cerridwen and Gwion Bach sings of Arianrhod's qualities in the poems related to his birth. He claims to have spent:

> *"Myvi a vum dri chyuynod mewn karchar Arianrhod."*
> "I spent three sojourns in the prison of Arianrhod."[23]

In addition to the Bard another creatively expressive caste was and is of enormous importance to Welsh culture – the storyteller. On the surface this may seem uncomplex, a mere entertainer of sorts before our multi-media technologies beamed stories into our lives in ultra-high definition. But on the contrary, the storytellers of Wales have always evoked a deeper sense of the magical and conveyed meaning by use of a symbolic landscape hidden in the guise of stories. The term for a storyteller in Welsh is 'Cyfarwydd', and it is the understanding of this term that transforms the idea of an entertainer into something that is indicative of profound knowledge, significance and ancestral wisdom. The meaning of this word is often lost in modern translations of the Four Branches of the Mabinogi, with one example of compelling note. In the text of the Fourth Branch, we are told that:

> *"Mi a dywedaf gyfarwydyd yn llawen. Ynteu Wydyon goreu kyfarwyd yn y byt oed."*[24]
> (I will gladly recite a tale. For he, Gwydion was the best 'cyfarwydd' in the world.)[25]

The term for storyteller is noted as 'cyfarwydd', with the word 'cyfarwydydd' used to refer to a story or a tale. In most translations, this term is simply interpreted as 'storyteller', but in doing so a hoard of magical connections are lost. To consult the *Geiriadur Prifysgol Cymru* (Dictionary of the Welsh Language), further meaning can be deduced. According to its interpretation the meaning of 'Cyfarwydd' is as follows:

> *"Cyfarwydd [cyf-arwydd] < Brth. Kom-are-ueid. Hysbys, cynefin, gwybodus, hyddysg, profiadol, celfydd, cywrain, medrus, adnabyddus, hyddysg mewn dewiniaeth."*
>
> *Well informed, acquainted, familiar, learned, versed, skilful, proficient, well known, skilled in magic*
>
> *"Chwedleuwr, ystorïwr, adroddwr chwedlau er diddanwch, gŵr wrth ei grefft gynt yn difyrru â chwedlau:"*
>
> *story-teller.*[26]

What will be notable in the above interpretation is that magic is inexorably fused not only into the fabric of story, but also in its dissemination. The primary meaning for Cyfarwydd concerns skills and knowledge, particularly those of magic. It is the secondary definition that states the term also applies to the storyteller. What sense can we make of this?

The Cyfarwyddion[27] were essentially powerful magicians, their function worked on three distinct levels – to entertain, to preserve culture, and to ensorcell their audience. To glean this understanding is to have one's assumption transformed, what may on the surface of modern bias be perceived as someone who entertains is transmuted by hidden depth of meaning. We would be foolhardy to consider the magical function of the Cyfarwydd to be a quality relegated to the past. Consider my earlier hypothesis of living a myth within a moment, the role of the Cyfarwydd today is essentially the same – to bring myth and story into an immanent experience in the present. Magic and story cannot be separated, in Welsh culture they are two sides of the same coin.

It is the divine fusion of Bard and Cyfarwydd that weave the stories of the gods and goddesses into the present, they are the benefactors of wisdom that have gifted the present with a deep magic. It is the function of modern Bards and storytellers to perpetuate this wisdom and knowledge.

Mysteries of the Mabinogi

The most famed account of Aranrhod's story is to be found in the Fourth Branch of the Mabinogi. These form a part of a collection of native tales collectively called The Mabinogion, they consist of eleven tales that are unique to Wales, whilst containing several identifiable international motifs, meaning they share a commonality with other world myths. They do this by employing various themes that have a universality to them and can be found worldwide, this suggests that mythology has a propensity to connect peoples and places that are at great distances apart. In doing so they express a human connection that is simultaneously mysterious and wondrous.

The first four tales within the Mabinogion collection are called 'Pedeir Ceinc y Mabinogi' (the Four Branches of the Mabinogi), since each branch ends with a sentence that reads –

> *"ac yuelly y teruyna y geing honn o'r Mabinogy."*
> "and here ends this branch of the Mabinogi."

The collection is found in two ancient manuscripts listed previously as – the *White Book of Rhydderch* dating to approximately 1350CE, and the *Red Book of Hergest,* dated at some time between 1382 and 1410CE. The term Mabinogion is a scribal error perpetuated and popularised by the pen of Lady Charlotte Guest, who offered one of the first translations of the collection in the English language, it is thought that she believed

Mabinogion to be the pleural of Mabinogi.[28] In her defence the manuscript she consulted contains a scribal error whereby the redactor seemingly chose to rhyme the final word of the first branch with a word in the previous sentence thus offering the term Mabynnogyon.[29]

Whilst many have speculated as to the meaning of the term 'Mabinogi', it is likely to be a reference to 'youth' or a 'story of youth', derived from the Welsh word 'mab' meaning boy or son. Early 20th century scholars expounded theories that the 'mab' component was derived from the British and Gaulish god Maponos. A hypothesis was suggested that the term pertains to a collection of stories indicative of the god Maponos, or the divine child.[30]

Whilst the Mabinogion collection is recorded on parchment, these tales existed in the oral storytelling tradition of Wales for centuries prior to their penning. Fragments of these stories can be found recorded in earlier material and within the poetic Bardic tradition of Wales. This suggests that there was not one penman, nobody claimed ownership of the material, it existed as an aspect of the collective memory of the people. These are cultural treasures that contain complexities that are often difficult to comprehend outside of said culture. The material offers clues as to their antiquity with certain themes hinting at a particular point in time. Some scholars have been forward in their hypothesis, others less so. Will Parker in his *The Four Branches of the Mabinogi* suggests that everything within them is rooted in the pre-Christian past.[31] He is not alone in this theory, Brynley Roberts in his introduction to the modern Welsh language edition of the Mabinogion collection suggests that they contain evolved versions of an ancient British pantheon of deities.[32] Modern scholar and Mabinogion expert, Sioned Davies corroborates these themes by asserting that the action within the tales is in pre-Christian Wales and suggests that the main characters are mythological figures whose counterparts can be found in ancient Britain.[33]

Many of these academics and scholars were influenced by other works and experts who went before them, and whilst some of those works are now outdated, their influence can still be felt. If I return momentarily to the previous work by Sir Ifor Williams, he made a rather bold statement about the era and timing of the tales when he said –

> *"Nid oes Sais na Norman i'w weld yn unman, eithr Brân yn frenin ar yr holl ynys, â choron Llundain ar ei ben. Nid yw'r Rhufeiniaid chwaith wedi cyrraedd, ond maent yn ymyl. Cyfnod y Mabinogi felly, ym meddwl y Cyfarwydd, ydoedd y cyfnod yn union o flaen dyfodiad cyntaf y Rhufeiniaid i'r ynys...Gan hynny, gwyddai chwedlydd y Mabinogi mai am cyfnod paganaidd cyn Crist yr oedd y sôn."*

> "There is no Englishman or Norman to be seen anywhere, and Brân is king of the whole island, with the crown of London upon his head. The Romans have not yet arrived either, but they are close by. Therefore, the period of the Mabinogi, in the mind of the storyteller, was the period directly before the first arrival of the Romans to this island...Therefore, the Mabinogi teller knew that he was talking about a pre-Christian pagan period."[34]

Whilst syncretically medieval in expression, it is generally accepted that the tales of the Mabinogion collection indicate a pre-Roman and pre-Christian origin. What is important to note is that whilst several academics, scholars and layman alike have claimed that the figures that populate the Mabinogion are echoes of an ancient British pantheon, it is imperative that the modern-day polytheist understands that these inhabitants in their current iteration were not worshipped as gods – as far as we can determine. To make this statement is not to dismiss them entirely, on the contrary, what we identify today as gods and goddesses are best described as Welsh deities. They have evolved and developed as deities in response to the needs of the people by various processes. The function of apotheosis has breathed life into the characters and awakened the echo of the divine within them. They are appropriate for today, and whilst many of them have counterparts in the deep past, it is their relevance to today that is of importance to the polytheist.

Whilst Arianrhod may be an echo of a distant deity, it is not helpful for the modern polytheist to obsessively stress over who she may have been, she is her own agency in the modern world. She is a Welsh goddess, perfectly evolved for the needs of the people today, and to express her virtues and attributes in a manner that enables and allows meaningful connection.

But what can the mythology tell us about her?

Chapter 3

The Mabinogi of Math, Son of Mathonwy
(A synopsis)

A wand that was bent to make you their own,
But your spirit remains, a lady unknown.
You hold the still point, the axis of life,
Spinner of wonder, of love and of strife.

Oh, goddess of fortune, guide me through,
Bring to me wisdom, reveal what is true.
The fates that turn the wheels of time,
In your wisdom I'll find what is truly mine.

Math the son of Mathonwy is High King of Gwynedd a Kingdom in the northwest of Wales. He is fated to always have his feet in the lap of a virgin unless he is at war. A young maiden named Goewin accompanies Math wherever he roams to ensure his feet are held in her lap. Math's nephew Gilfaethwy falls obsessively in love with Goewin and cunningly plans a plot with his brother Gwydion to have her as his own. Gwydion helps his brother and starts a war so that Math can be separated from Goewin, leaving her vulnerable to Gilfaethwy. Gwydion petitions his Uncle Math to allow him to journey to south Wales with eleven men to ask for the pigs that Pryderi has, and which originally came from the Welsh otherworld – Annwfn. Disguised as poets, the band of men sing at Pryderi's court in return for a fee – the pigs of Annwfn. Pryderi declines, and in turn Gwydion offers him the finest steeds and hounds and all their accoutrements. Unbeknown to Pryderi the animals are created by magical means, taking the pigs Gwydion and Gilfaethwy return to Gwynedd. The enchanted steeds and hounds and all their accoutrements, now separated from Gwydion's powers return to their former shapes. Pryderi declares war on Math and the Kingdom of Gwynedd, who leaves Goewin to focus on his army.

Gwydion and Gilfaethwy find Goewin. Gilfaethwy has sex with Goewin against her will. The next day the brothers travel with Math to face Pryderi's army. A great massacre on each side takes place. Pryderi's southern forces are beaten and begin to retreat. Pryderi tries to make peace and challenges Gwydion to single combat to settle the issue. Gwydion kills Pryderi and the war ends.

When Math returns home Goewin tells him that she is no longer a virgin and that she had been defiled by his nephews – Gilfaethwy and Gwydion, and in that act, they shamed him also. Math takes Goewin as his wife to compensate her for the shame of being raped by his nephews. He punishes them by transforming them into different animals. First, he turns Gilfaethwy into a female deer and Gwydion into a stag so that they must live together and mate with each other and take on the nature of the wild animals. Within a year they have mated and bear young, and then return to Math to be transformed into another type of animal. Math strikes them with his wand, and the one who was a hind becomes a wild boar, and the one who was a stag became a wild sow.

The offspring was taken and transformed into boy which Math baptised and fostered. A year and a day later the animals return with another offspring, he strikes the offspring turning him into an auburn-haired lad. He then strikes the one who had been a wild boar into a she-wolf, and the one who had been a wild sow into a wolf. They live in the guise of these animals for a year and return to Math with a third offspring that he transforms into a young boy. With their punishment at an end, Gwydion and Gilfaethwy are returned to their former selves.

Having lost his foot holder, Math must find a new maiden to fulfil his fate. Gwydion recommends his sister Aranrhod the daughter of Dôn to be Math's new foot holder. Math tests her virginity by making her jump over his magic wand which he bends and places on the ground before her. As she jumps, a large, sturdy, yellow-haired boy drops from within her. Aranrhod flees for the door but immediately but drops a small something. Gwydion secretly collects the object and hides it in a chest in his chambers. Math names the yellow-haired boy Dylan. After Dylan is baptized, he takes to the sea and vanishes, becoming a part of the sea by taking on its nature.

One day whilst in his chambers Gwydion hears a cry from the chest at the foot of the bed and discovers that the thing that Aranrhod dropped from her body has turned into a boy. He raises the boy in secret and when the child was four years old, he took him to Caer Aranrhod and introduces the boy as her son. Aranrhod is furious and rejects his claims because of the shame she feels. In her anger she asks for the boy's name, to which Gwydion replies that he does not have one. In her fury she swears a destiny upon the boy that he will never have a name unless given to him by her. Gwydion by use of magic transforms himself and the boy into the finest shoemakers and tricks Aranrhod to name the boy – Lleu Llaw Gyffes (fair one of the skilful hand).

When she discovers the magical deception, in her fury, she swears another fate upon the child, that he shall never bear weapons until armed by herself. However, Gwydion's takes to magic once more and forces Aranrhod's hand in giving arms to the child. Aranrhod in her anger and shame places a third destiny upon the chid that her son that he will never have a wife of the race of the earth.

By then Lleu had grown into a handsome man but unable to marry. And so, Gwydion and Math took to their magic and conjured a woman from flowers and named her Blodeu(w)edd,[35] meaning 'of flowers'. Lleu marries Blodeu(w)edd and Math bequeaths them their own lands. One day Lleu leaves to visit Math when a nobleman named Gronw Pebr passes through the lands on a hunt. He meets Blodeu(w)edd and they fall deeply in love. Gronw and Blodeu(w)edd plot to kill Lleu so that they can be together. Lleu cannot be killed by ordinary means and Blodeu(w)edd uses her husband's trust to find out how to overcome the protective spells which prevent his death. After a year of hard work, Gronw can mortally wound Lleu and escape with Blodeu(w)edd. Lleu does not immediately die and instead transforms into an eagle and flies away. Gwydion, by following a mysterious sow seeks Lleu out and finds him rotting in the form of an eagle in the topmost branches of the Tree of Life. He sings a song-spell to Lleu to summon him from the tree and turns him back into his human form. In time, the frail Lleu recovers from his ordeal. He seeks out compensation from Gronw with Gwydion and the backing of Math's army.

Blodeu(w)edd hears of the army's imminent arrival to punish her for her wrongdoing. She tries to flee with her maidens, but Gwydion catches her and causes the drowning of all her maidens. He strikes her with his wand and transforms her into a bird that will be scorned by all other birds, and she becomes the first owl, destined to hunt only by night. In doing so he changes her name to Blodeu(w)edd meaning flower-face. Gronw offers Lleu land and money as compensation for his part in his attempted murder. Lleu refuses. He wants to return the blow which nearly killed him. Gronw accepts but then attempts to avoid his punishment by using a stone as a shield between him and the spear. Lleu agrees to his petition and throws the spear which pierces the stone and breaks Gronw's back, killing him immediately. The stone stands there to this day and is called Llech Gronw (the stone of Gronw). Lleu Llaw Gyffes repossesses his lands and ruled over them prosperously.

Chapter 4

The Analysis of Myth

Your eyes, like the stars, shine bright and clear,
Reflecting the mysteries as they draw near.
You are the still point, heart of the wheel,
The hub of all motion, the celestial reel.

Your hair, like galaxies, flows with grace,
A river of stars, a cosmic embrace.
Your voice, like the wind, whispers secrets of old,
Guiding my journey to mystery untold.

On first reading or hearing the tale, the Fourth Branch and the story of Aranrhod may evoke strong feelings in those reading her myth. Is she deceived, has she been set up by Gwydion or Math, what is going on under the surface? There are complex issues swimming within the myth, many of which are beyond the scope of this short book to explore fully. Therefore, the following discourse will focus primarily on the themes that are intimately tied to the mysteries of Aranrhod as they appear within the myth. This is not to exclude other figures whose stories and meaning have been in explored in other books within the Pagan Portals series.

The narrative of the Fourth Branch is replete with themes that resonate with contemporary audiences including ones that are highly emotive, covering diverse subjects from loyalty and parental obligations, to incest, rape, and several non-consensual actions that 21st Century audiences may find highly problematic. The struggle for power and the corrupting influence of desire are timeless motifs that add depth and complexity to the story, they can also inflame the reader or listener, and at times, these and other difficult themes can act as an insurmountable barrier for further exploration. Furthermore, the Fourth Branch explores the consequences of violating taboos and the importance of respecting the natural order of the world.

Math's fate and the corruption of order by proxy of the behaviour of Gwydion and Gilfaethwy serves as a warning about the dangers of ignoring the sacred laws that govern the world which we inhabit. And at the centre of it all is the enigmatic Aranrhod, whose actions may on the surface of things appear bewildering or contrary to her assumed nature. A series of events take place before we are introduced to Aranrhod, and whilst these may initially appear to steer us away from her exploration, they are a necessary prelude to her introduction. In understanding the events that set up the scenes of the Fourth Branch we glean an insight into the mechanism of myth that preserve the memory of Aranrhod.

The Defilement of Goewin

The brothers Gwydion and Gilfaethwy are the initial driving forces that instigate the turmoil required to bring Aranrhod into the narrative. The deceit of the brothers in succeeding to defile Goewin results in a temporary displacement of balance and power that must be rectified for the status quo to be re-established. The initial sequence of events appears to be brutal and horrific, making any thought of finding meaning or wisdom a difficult task. And yet, meaning does indeed lie beneath the sequence of events that occur to bring Aranrhod into the mix of myth. Aranrhod's involvement in the narrative is a direct result of the raping of Goewin, and, however, uncomfortable and triggering we must delve into this seemingly horrendous event to discover the mechanism of mystery at work.

Goewin's name means 'daring and bold', and her role in the Fourth Branch occupies a common function in ancient Welsh culture, one of the '*troediog*' – the foot-holder of the King, and whilst the role has a courtly reality, it is apparent that in the narrative it has been mythologised. According to the Welsh codex the function of the *troediog* was to – *'ef a dely daly trayt e brenin en y arfet'* (he would hold the feet of the king in his lap), with the word *arfet* rendered into modern Welsh as *arffed* meaning the groin or lap.[36] However, in the Fourth Branch the terminology used is different in that Math's survival was dependant on his feet being – *'ymlyc croth morwyn'* (within, or in the folds of a maiden's womb).[37] The original language used is considerably more visceral than that found in translation, which most often renders the term *'croth'* (meaning womb, uterus, abdomen and belly) as simply 'lap'. What meaning can we deduce from the original language?

The choice of words is not by accident, but entirely by design. We are informed at the commencement of the Fourth Branch that the King cannot live lest his feet be in the womb or belly of a maiden, note that it is the term *'morwyn'* that is used in the original Welsh, which does not translate exclusively to virgin, in fact its use to denote a virgin is mostly in reference to Mary the mother of Christ. The primary meaning of *'morwyn'* is a female attendant, a maid, or an unmarried young girl.[38] Whilst questions of virginity appear to be central to the myth, this is not as clear cut as one might initially believe. The situation is significantly more nuanced than it appears, the term morwyn does not exclusively refer to virginity but more so to a state of innocence and purity, or to a woman who is not betrothed to a man. What can be established with certainty is that Goewin's role is that of the King's foot-holder, but this requires a deeper dive.

If we look to the laws of medieval Wales, impeccably recorded in a body of work called 'The Laws of Hywel Dda' from the 12th century and purported to have been initially compiled in the 10th century by King Hywel Dda (Hywel the Good), we will note a curiosity that is worthy of examination. The role of the foot-holder is recorded as a junior member of the court, and one who is entitled to his lands for free, to a horse, plus woollen clothing that would be given to him by the King and fine linen by the Queen. The law states that the foot-holder is required to hold the Kings feet in his lap from when he commences his court or when he is sitting to banquet until the moment that he takes to his chambers.[39] In addition, the foot-holder would do his utmost to protect the King from harm. For his duties the foot-holder would also receive a wage.

What is apparent in the description of the law is that the foot-holder is gendered as male, this was a position that a boy or a man would undertake and not a woman. However, in the myth it genders the foot-holder as female. A medieval audience would have been familiar with these courtly customs and this shift in gender roles may well have highlighted to them that things were not as they obviously appeared. The flipping of gender roles is a particular oddity within the Fourth Branch that will be explored later.

Goewin's role as foot-holder and the fact that Math's survival is dependent on his feet being in her womb can be perceived as the necessity for the King to be betrothed to the land itself. Math is presented as an unmarried King, i.e., he does not have a Queen as a consort, instead his survival is entirely reliant on his feet being held by the womb of the divine feminine. Can this be interpreted as a symbolic form of intercourse? If so, then the necessity for the foot-holder to be a virgin is defunct and something else is happening beneath the currents of story. Goewin represents the sovereignty goddess of the land and is essentially the first element of the divine feminine we are introduced to in the Fourth Branch. As previously noted, Goewin's name means she who is daring and bold, but how does this tie into the quality of the goddess of the land?

Goewin embodies qualities that are integral to the well-being and prosperity of the kingdom of Gwynedd. The meaning of her name reflects attributes that are essential for a sovereign figure in a mythological context, in other words the King must emulate the qualities that the name Goewin expresses.

The King is responsible for protection of the land, and as sovereign must be courageous to protect the land from external threats. In mythological narratives, the land often faces dangers from invaders, mythical creatures, or internal strife and tribulations. A daring and bold sovereign is necessary to confront and overcome these challenges, ensuring that the land remains safe and prosperous. Courage is also essential in upholding justice. In the Mabinogi, rulers are often faced with difficult moral decisions and conflicts and otherworldly forces that may not be immediately obvious. A sovereign imbued with boldness would have the fortitude to make just decisions and enforce laws, maintaining order and harmony within their realm. Boldness can signify a willingness to innovate and drive progress forwards. In a mythical context, the prosperity of the land is often linked to the wisdom and forward-thinking nature of its leaders, and we can assume that the prosperity of Gwynedd was secure in Math's capable hands, that is until the status-quo was disrupted.

Boldness is also a marker of resilience. The land, and by extension its sovereign, must endure and recover from hardships such as natural disasters, famines, tribal conflict and wars. A bold sovereign embodies the resilience and tenacity needed to lead the land through difficult times and emerge from it stronger. Within the Mabinogi the land is seen as a living entity, in modern polytheism this entity is often personified by a goddess or a female figure. The qualities of daring and boldness could reflect the divine power and favour necessary for a ruler to be seen as legitimate and thus blessed by the goddess. A bold goddess would imply a land imbued with divine strength and vitality, qualities that we see emulated in Math.

Boldness and daring can also be symbolic of fertility and the vigorous life force of the land itself. A sovereign goddess who embodies these qualities might be seen as ensuring the land's fertility, leading to bountiful harvests and the flourishing of both nature and society. When we are introduced to Goewin we can safely assume that this is the status-quo, all is as it should be, that is until the natural order is disrupted by the actions of the two brothers. Goewin's role as the King's foot-holder and her attributes can be seen as a reflection of the high esteem in which women and goddesses were held. They were not passive figures but active participants in the maintenance and prosperity of the land. However, the King and the goddess do not create offspring as such, instead the influence of their pairing is the general fertility and fruition of the land and its inhabitants, human and otherwise.

As this book has demonstrated by the complexity of Arianrhod's name, personal nouns in Welsh mythology are often deeply symbolic, conveying the quiddity of a character. Goewin's name directly connects her to the qualities needed for sovereignty to be embodied and then emulated by the King. By being daring and bold, she personifies the proactive and resilient spirit necessary for the well-being of the land. Goewin reflects a multifaceted view of what it means to be a sovereign. It highlights the need for courage, resilience, innovation, and the seeking of divine favour in ensuring the land's prosperity. These attributes, in turn, mirror the nature of a goddess who is not merely a passive entity but an active, powerful force essential for the health and vitality of the land. It is the function of storytelling that humanises these concepts into the vulnerable figure that we are introduced to. But as we have seen, we would be foolhardy to consider her as exclusively human.

All of this offers an intriguing glimpse into the potential pre-Christian relationship that the King had with the earth itself. For fertility of the land to be guaranteed the King must be betrothed to the sovereignty of earth. For Math's sovereignty to be successful he had to be intimately connected, if not symbolically betrothed to the goddess. This implies a reciprocity where the goddess chooses the king, and in turn this ritual union is reflected in the prosperity and fertility of the Kingdom. Celtic scholar, John Carey, offers an intriguing hypothesis that the tale of Math is a creation myth of sorts, in which is expressed a relationship with the land that represented a time before a marriage between King and goddess was necessary, a time before the 'fall' into mortality and morality where men simply stood upon the earth or rested their feet upon her. If this situation endured there would be no death, the King and his people would survive.[40]

Whilst Carey's theory is intriguing and perhaps his observations of a 'before time' are correct, for the polytheist the relationship between King and goddess can offer a pertinence that can deepen our understanding of the myth and how to glean wisdom from it. The connection between Math and Goewin has an underlying tension, it is a necessity, and only strife and war can safely remove the King from the womb of the goddess. It is the deceit of Gwydion and Gilfaethwy that initiates a battle of such magnitude that Math must intervene, thus leaving Goewin in a vulnerable position. Her defiling can be seen as a desecration of the earth itself, and of the natural order of things, in this capacity Gwydion and Gilfaethwy occupy a curious position as the expression of humanity's crimes against the natural laws of the earth herself. Within these two figures we can perhaps see our own behaviour and actions that cause harm to a planet that feeds and nurtures us. What results is a state of flux, where the status-quo is shattered, sovereignty is diminished, and chaos ensues. The King has no option but to do the right thing and marry Goewin, thus removing her from the position of sovereignty goddess into mortal Queen. The resulting dangerous void could potentially cause untold damage to the apparent world and its inhabitants unless the

King can yet again place his feet in the womb of a sovereignty goddess – setting the stage for Aranrhod to enter the narrative.

The Influence of the Otherworld and the Arrival of Aranrhod

It is easy to fall into the trap of assuming and believing that the myth is referring to actual people, ones who may have occupied a real place in the distant past – but to do so would dismiss the nuance of myth. Various events happen within the myth that inform the listener that things are not as they appear, and at a certain point in the narrative the audience would have been acutely aware of otherworldly forces entering the story. These details can easily be missed by the modern reader, unaccustomed with the hidden symbolism of culture and its mythologies.

The initial paragraphs of the Fourth Branch position the events in the Kingdom of Gwynedd, a real place that exists to this day in northwest Wales. The Kings' court is mentioned by name, albeit there is no archaeological evidence to pinpoint its location, and then we are offered the description of the foot-holder which defies the laws of Hywel Dda. Within a few short lines, what was initially set in the apparent world descends into an ethereal place betwixt and between. This liminal state is heightened when the influence of the indigenous otherworld breaks through into the narrative, and this occurs with the mention of pigs.

For Goewin to be left unattended by Math, Gwydion sets about to steal supernatural pigs from the Kingdom of Pryderi in the South of Wales. These pigs were given to Pryderi's father Pwyll in the First Branch of the Mabinogi, they act as primary symbols of Otherworldly forces. It is the first instance where a medieval audience would have been aware that nothing from this point on would be straightforward or obvious. This is a vital tool for the modern polytheist and mythologist, to look for instances when otherworldly forces break through into the story. This creates another level of tension and a dynamic which can be easily missed and lost in translation. As soon as the pigs enter the Kingdom of Gwynedd all familiarity is lost, only the names of places bear any semblance to the apparent world. Everything from this point onwards exists in a state of profound flux, where the powerful forces of the Otherworld are bleeding into our world, challenging, teaching, initiating crisis and healing all at once. In essence, the overlaying of the Otherworld onto the apparent realm transforms the myth from a mere story to a profound metaphor for life, and an opportunity to glean deep spiritual wisdom.

From this perspective, a young woman from the Kingdom of Gwynedd has not been defiled, it is the earth herself that has been insulted and desecrated, and it is humanity that is to blame. The arrival of Aranrhod within the supernatural element of the tale is an attempt to restore balance, but this is myth, and even then, things are not as they appear. For since the arrival of the pigs in Gwynedd, we have entered the realm of gods, demigods, their exploits and adventures. The stage for transformation has been set.

Our introduction to Aranrhod in the Fourth Branch comes via her brother, Gwydion and his attempt to reconcile with his uncle in providing a suitable maiden to act as foot-holder for the King. The character of Gwydion is particularly fascinating, as he embodies contradictory qualities that are simultaneously horrific, appalling, heroic and selfless. His cunning, intelligence, and magical abilities make him a formidable force in the kingdom of Gwynedd. On the other hand, his loyalty to his brother resulting in the defilement of an innocent can cause the reader to loathe and detest him as a character. His role in the story serves as a counterpoint to the destructive forces unleashed by Gilfaethwy's actions and his attempts at reconciliation, highlighting the importance of wisdom, courage, and honour, and standing up and taking responsibility for one's actions. It is almost impossible to explore the nature of Aranrhod without referring to Gwydion, they are inexorably linked, not only as siblings, but as magical forces that drive the function of the myth forwards.

Throughout the Fourth Branch, Aranrhod is presented as Gwydion's antagonist, with every aspect of her story woven into his actions. Because of this we would be remiss to consider that Aranrhod exists in a vacuum, she does not, she is an intricate part of a delicate yet powerful weaving of several forces that are reliant upon each other to drive the myth onwards. This is true of any individual, we are not islands, but part of a delicate yet complex web of interconnections.

Before we delve further into the relationship between Aranrhod and Gwydion it is pertinent for us to consider if there is a connection between Aranrhod and the one she is meant to replace. When we are initially introduced to Aranrhod all mention of Goewin depart the narrative, yet we would be foolish to consider that she no longer serves a purpose. Whilst Goewin and Aranrhod are distinct characters, each with their different roles, there are intriguing thematic and symbolic connections apparent between them that may suggest a deeper mythological relationship, or perhaps a shared origin in earlier traditions. Both figures hold roles that are tied to sovereignty and sacred order and balance, Goewin expresses the inherent sovereignty of the land, whilst Aranrhod represents the still point at the centre that maintains order even amidst chaos. Goewin's role as foot-holder is directly connected to Math's Kingship and indicates a symbiotic relationship between King and the land itself. In turn, Aranrhod's actions influence the line of succession and the legitimacy of her offspring, the inherent nature of which are also brought into question and in their examination further mystery can be discovered.

On the surface of things, virginity and purity appear as crucial aspects in the role of both figures. Goewin's violation disrupts the Kingdom's order, necessitating a quest for restoration, one which Gwydion attempts to repair and in turn reconcile with Math. Aranrhod's failed virginity test reveals hidden truths and sets in motion significant events that not only affect the Kingdom for narrative purposes but also reveal profound mysteries. When we consider both figures in unison it is evident that they are responsible for processes of transformation and change. Goewin's defilement and subsequent marriage to Math leads to a reordering of the court of Gwynedd, while Aranrhod's later challenges to her son Lleu ultimately lead to his growth and empowerment and the restoration of the Kingdom. Given the symbolic weight and thematic connections present, it is plausible that Goewin and Aranrhod represent different aspects of a single mythological archetype or goddess figure, each one embodying facets of sovereignty, purity, and transformation, each responsible for maintaining sacred and natural order.

Goewin might represent the foundational, nurturing aspect of sovereignty that is tied to the land's purity and order, while Aranrhod embodies the transformative, challenging aspect, bringing about change and renewal through her actions. In this guise each figure represents two sides of the same coin, the loving and the vengeful mother – in Goewin we see the benevolent face of the goddess as an aspect of the earth itself, its fertility and prosperity. In Aranrhod we meet harshness, coldness verging on vindictiveness that betrays the very nature of motherhood, and yet without her intervention the child – Lleu – would never be transformed. In this manner Aranrhod parallels the actions of Cerridwen as terrible and vengeful mother or the stepmother of Culhwch in the epic tale of Culhwch ac Olwen. In all instances the vengeful mother initiates a quest by means of a fate that is bestowed upon the child. Without this aspect of the vengeful mother, the story would not progress. Her actions express a sense of purpose and function that may not be immediately and obviously apparent, leading us to judge and condemn her for what may appear to be bewildering and perplexing decisions. So, whilst Goewin and Aranrhod might appear as distinct characters in the myth their thematic connections suggest that they may reflect different aspects of a deeper mythological concept, perhaps originating from a shared archetype related to sovereignty, purity, and transformation.

Aranrhod's arrival is the consequence of the defilement of the earth goddess, she is the result of years of chaos that brought about a breakdown of order, her appearance in the myth is an attempt to return a state of balance. But for this to occur – what is initially broken must be fixed – and that which is broken is the human spirit, defiled by its own actions. As we have seen, Gwydion and Gilfaethwy's abhorrent behaviour are a metaphor for the human defilement of the earth and her resources and a corruption of the human condition. Math is subsequently without a foot-holder and the relationship between human sovereignty and that of the earth begins to break down into chaos. This state of flux creates a dangerous liminal period where balance is at stake. Aranrhod in the guise of the vengeful mother and as the sacred axle is an attempt to restore the balance of the wheels that have been upturned by Goewin's defilement. For this to be achieved a new child must be born, and in its birthing a process of initiation and transformation occurs to restore balance to the human spirit that has been corrupted. It initiates a quest in search of the true self, and this is expressed through the offspring of Aranrhod. This may sound somewhat akin to a saviour complex; however, it does not refer to single saviour figure like the Christ child of the Christian religion, but rather to the illumination of all nature's children, a return to innocence and symbiosis with nature.

A Question of Paternity

Perhaps the most perplexing aspect of the myth is not only the sudden arrival of Aranrhod but her willingness to participate in a virginity test that she subsequently fails. In this failing she births twins, albeit one is unformed at the time of its birthing. Questions of paternity have plagued scholar and lay person alike since these myths were popularised in the modern world. In the following pages we shall delve not only in to the nature of parentage but also discover the nature of the children that are birthed at the court of Math.

It is assumed, almost by default that Gwydion is the father of Aranrhod's offspring, and on the surface of things this may make some sense, but as we delve deeper into the matter you will find that things are not as clear cut. Aranrhod's response to the shame that Gwydion has brought upon her give credence to an incestual relationship between herself and her brother, and yet at no point does Gwydion admit to paternity. His actions on the other hand may betray the fact that he is the child's father because he becomes a surrogate parent, a role that would have been highly unusual in Medieval Wales, and one that would have struck the audience as odd.

However, various discrepancies are evidently present that questions the paternity of Gwydion. The first and perhaps most obvious is that prior to suggesting Aranrhod for the position of foot-holder, Gwydion was in animal form for three years and three days, during which his entire *anian* – or inherent nature had been transformed into that of each animal he and his brother occupied. During this time, not a single aspect of their humanity remained intact. Gwydion had not had any interactions with Aranrhod for over three years, so how would he have been aware of the status of her virginity? In turn, whilst her shaming is mentioned in another text as significant, she never once spells out the nature of that shame, at no point does she nor Gwydion suggest that he is the father, and that the child is the result of incest.

If we look carefully at the myth and the language used, we can glean surprising clarity as to the true father of Aranrhod's offspring. In the first instance the clue is purely symbolic. Aranrhod is brought to the court of Math where he enquires of the state of her innocence and purity –

> *"A forwyn," heb ef, "a wyt forwyn di?"*
> "Maiden," said he, "are you a virgin?"

To which she replies…

> *"Ni wnn i amgen no'm bot."*
> I know of no reason why I should not be."

This rather cryptic reply by Aranrhod is peculiar for surely, she would have known if she was indeed a virgin or not. Or is this episode merely questioning a state of innocence or attempting to discern if she is unmarried as the term *morwyn* implies? In turn Math's response to her reply initiates a symbolic and magical union with immediate results as the text sates –

> *"Yna y kymerth ynteu yr hutlath a'y chamu. "Camha di dros honn," heb ef, "ac os wyt forwyn, mi a ednebydaf." Yna y camawd hitheu dros yr hutlath, ac ar y cam hwnnw, adaw mab brasuelyn mawr a oruc. Sef a wnaeth y mab, dodi diaspat uchel. Yn ol diaspat y mab, kyrchu y drws a oruc hi, ac ar hynny adaw y ryw bethan ohonei. A chyn cael o neb guelet yr eil olwc arnaw, Gwydion a'y kymerth, ac a droes llen o bali yn y gylch, ac a'e cudyawd.'"*

> "Then he took the magic wand and bent it upwards. "Step over this," he said, "and if you are a maiden, I will know it." Then she stepped over the magic wand, and in that step, she dropped a large boy with curly yellow hair. What the boy did was give a loud cry. After the boy's cry, she made for the door, and as she went, she dropped a

> small something. Before anyone could get a second look at it, Gwydion picked it up and wrapped it in a sheet of brocaded silk and hid it."

Whilst evidently phallic in its symbology, the Welsh language gives further credence to this in its use of the word *'hutlath'* which is used figuratively to mean penis. A subtlety of language is often overlooked in this episode. If we look closely at the words used –

> *'Yna y kymerth ynteu yr hutlath a'y chamu. "Camha di dros honn,"*

You will note that the words *chamu* and *camha* are remarkably similar, and for good reason, the Cyfarwydd is playing with the magic of words. The narrator uses the verbal noun 'chamu' (camu in modern Welsh) to imply a bending upwards of the wand. However, the spoken imperative 'camha' instigates an interesting juxtaposition between these two words. They intimately connect the actions of both Math and Aranrhod, with the latter opening her legs as she steps over the proxy penis. In previous episodes the wand has been used to strike an object or person to change it, here the symbolism is obviously sexual in nature.[41]

Math bends his wand upwards implying a form of erection, over which Aranrhod steps. The result is immediate, and startling and she births a large boy with curly yellow hair. As the boy cried loudly Aranrhod took to leaving, dropping as she did another small thing in her wake. Did Math impregnate Aranrhod in that instant causing her to immediately give birth or might there be some other hidden meaning and mystery held in this sequence?

Having considered the connection between Goewin and Aranrhod, one suggestion might be that Goewin is indeed pregnant either with the seed of Gilfaethwy who defiled her, or that of Math her husband/King. The gestation of Gilfaethwy's offspring would have been over three years long, presenting a ludicrous twist in the narrative. But Math's *Hudlath* (wand) has the power not only to change the shape and form of an object or individual but also its inherent essence suggests that he has immense power. The episode with Aranrhod can be seen as the transferring of the children from the womb of Goewin as injured sovereignty of the land to the womb of the vengeful mother, who by processes of initiation redeems the human spirit and reinstates the natural order. This would imply that Goewin conceives the children whilst it is Aranrhod that gives birth to them, albeit she renounces any motherly responsibility for them. If this is the case, then Math is acutely conscious of what mechanisms are at play, and for the chaos of the previous three years to be restored a new order must be conceived.

The shift in gears within the mechanism of the story is obvious, and yet given little notice or attention in modern retellings and dissections. The matter of the King's foot-holder and the reestablishing of order does not occur, a suitable maiden is not found, therefore the intention of the story has moved along both in narrative terms and in meaning. When we stop to take notice of this, we can detect the truth of what is occurring beneath the lines of narrative.

As Aranrhod escapes the court and makes for the door having dropped a large curly haired boy, Math says something rather peculiar which is often lost in translation –

> *"Ie," heb Math fab Mathonwy, "mi a baraf uedydyaw hwn," wrth y mab brasuelyn. "Sef enw a baraf, Dylan.".*
>
> "Yes," Said Math son of Mathowny, "I will have this one baptised." Referring to the large yellow haired boy. "And the name I have prepared for him is Dylan."

I draw your attention to the word *'baraf'* in the original language, which is a mutation of the word *'paraf'*. In general, within English translations, this word is glossed over in preference for the translation of – the name I will give him is Dylan. In this oversimplification we lose the nuance of the word *'baraf'*. In its fullest form the word means to create, fashion or form, to change the state or quality of a person or a thing, to cause, to bring about, to make ready or to prepare. The meaning of this word fits into the function of Math as we have come to understand him, his magical abilities are of such magnitude that he has the power to change the shape, form and inherent quality or essence of a thing or a person. A task that he undertook when transforming the brothers, Gwydion and Gilfaethwy into different animals. It implies that Math had a name already prepared and in mind for this child – but how can that be the case? The narrative hints that Math was not aware of the imminent arrival of the child and small thing. And yet, the words used contradicts this to imply that Math did in fact know exactly what was happening.

The function of baptism is interesting as is the choice of words, when Math instructs that the child is to be baptised it is tempting to associate the term with that of the Christian tradition of baptism. Baptism rituals in the Mabinogi and wider Welsh mythology appears to have three defined functions. According to Sir Ifor Williams, the baptism ritual within the Mabinogi is significant of naming a child rather than dedicating or blessing it to a particular deity and has elements of Paganism rather than Christianity.[42] Its other function is to place the nature and meaning of that name upon the personality, a magical act that changes the inherent essence of the child to match its name. Thirdly, the act of baptism and the pouring of water on or over the head is a method by which the child or individual is inducted or re-inducted back into society. We see a clear example of this earlier in the Fourth Branch, when the punishment of Gwydion and Gilfaethwy is completed, Math instructs that they are to have their heads wetted and dressed in fine clothing. In other words, they are re-introduced into the world of humans after living as animals for three years.

At the heart of all this is the power that Math wields, demonstrating that he is not simply a monarch but also a magician of great ability. As soon as the young boy is baptised and named another peculiarity occurs –

> *"Bedydyaw a wnaethpwyt y mab, ac y gyt ac y bedydywyt, y mor a gyrchwys. Ac yn y lle, y gyt ac y doeth y'r mor, annyan y mor a gauas."*
>
> "And so, they baptised the boy, and as soon as he was baptised, he made for the sea. And there, as soon as he came to the sea, the nature of the sea he became."

It is the word *annyan* (anian in modern Welsh) that is significant here, not only does Dylan take to the sea, in essence he becomes one with it. *Anian* refers to not only the inherent nature or quiddity of a person or thing but also refers to natural order and the laws of nature herself. Thus far we have seen how the natural order has been disrupted and corrupted by the actions of the two brothers. Therefore, Dylan can be seen as a symbol of the necessity for the re-establishment of natural order. Furthermore, the name Dylan means the sea, the ocean and the deep, and within the narrative it is said that a consequence of him taking on the nature of the sea he is subsequently called *'Dylan Eil Ton'*, or Sea, he of or son of the wave, for the Eil can be used metaphorically to mean son. Essentially Dylan is a metaphor for the undifferentiated consciousness of the sea itself, and Math is more than aware of this function.

We are getting closer now to understanding who the rightful father of the child and the small thing is, the one person who has the power to stabilise the forces that have been disrupted – Math.

If we look at the evidence thus far, Math uses his wand not only to transform the shape and form of his nephews but also to magically transfer the child and small thing from Goewin into the womb of Aranrhod. He names and baptises the child, a role that in Welsh law is afforded to the rightful parent. Baptism serves a function by which a child cannot be named by its name unless baptised as such. Math is later responsible for upturning one of Aranrhod's fates and creates a wife for Lleu, essentially Math gives Lleu his patrimony and Lleu eventually succeeds Math as Lord of Gwynedd. All this points in the direction of Math being the rightful father of the child and small thing that Aranrhod births. Further evidence for this is to be found in a collection of manuscripts from Medieval Wales that are worthy of brief exploration.

The Welsh have long been obsessed with genealogies, recording them in both legal texts and mythology, a collection of genealogies can be found in several medieval manuscripts compiled into a tome called Bonedd yr Arwyr (the nobility or gentry of heroes). The earliest copy of which was written sometime around the year 1475 and is designated as the National Library of Wales Peniarth Manuscript #131 and the Llanstephan Manuscript #28. These manuscripts may appear to be significantly later than the Mabinogi collection, but several scholars by analysing the language used have claimed that they may date to the same period, if not earlier than the Mabinogi. Celtic scholar Sarah Ziser claims that the Bonedd yr Arwyr demonstrates that earlier version of these tales probably existed and offered fuller versions of the tale of the house of Dôn and her family.[43]

The genealogies of the House of Dôn are listed thus –

Plant Dôn o Arfon – The Children of Dôn from Arfon[44]

{sons}

1. Gwydion
2. Govannon
3. Amaethon
4. Hunawg
5. Idwal
6. Jenuydd (Eufydd)
7. Elestron
8. Digant
9. Gylfaethwy
10. Kynnan
11. Hedd
12. Addien
13. Elawg

{daughter}

14. Aranrhod/Arianrhod[45]

In total, 14 offspring of Dôn are listed, five of which are named within the Fourth Branch of the Mabinogi. Elestron and Eufydd are also known to the Welsh tradition and are named in the *Book of Taliesin* poetry together with Math, Gwydion, Lleu and Gofannon. Of the remaining seven names no surviving manuscript records their names or their stories. The only daughter named as a child of Dôn is Aranrhod/ Arianrhod.

In addition, the genealogy continues in a surprising direction but one which gives further evidence to the paternity of Aranrhod's offspring –

Plant Math ap Mathonwy – The Children of Math son of Mathonwy

1. Lleu Llaw Gyffess
2. Dylan Eil Ton
3. and Blodeu(w)edd their sister, from Arianrhod the daughter of Dôn their mother.

These genealogical traits clearly state that the father of the three names listed is indeed Math the son of Mathonwy, high King of Gwynedd and powerful magician. The theme of incestual or unnatural coupling that is a common theme in the myths is maintained here, for Aranrhod is Math's niece. What might be surprising is that Math is also listed as the parent/father of Blodeu(w)edd. However, this makes sense when we consider that Gwydion asks his uncle to help him circumvent Aranrhod's fate that Lleu will not marry a woman that is currently of the race of the earth. In the *Book of Taliesin* epic poem – The Battle of the Trees – Taliesin compares his own birth to that of the flower maiden by saying –

> *"A'm swynwys i Fath, kyn bum diameth. A'm swynwys i Wydion, mawrut o brithron."*
>
> "By magic did Math create me, before I was completed. By magic did Gwydion fashion me, by might of his wand."[46]

This comparison positions Math as the father of Blodeu(w)edd, the initial creator, whereas it is Gwydion who is responsible for fashioning her into a suitable bride, again denoting the peculiar position of Gwydion defying gender roles by assuming a feminine parental role. Whilst many scholars and layperson alike have assigned the paternal role to Gwydion, the evidence from the several manuscripts compiled into Bonedd yr Arwyr suggest otherwise by clearly stating that it is indeed Math who is the rightful father.

Albeit the collection in Bonedd yr Arwyr is late, these names were likely understood by the Cyfarwyddon (storytellers) and the general populace of medieval Wales. If they had been compiled after the composition of the Four Branches then their contents would have reflected the relationships within that narrative, which they clearly do not. Therefore, they are likely referring to lost elements of the tale, and that loss has muddied the waters of the narrative, causing future readers and investigators of myth to incorrectly position Gwydion as the father of Dylan, Lleu and Blodeu(w)edd.

Chapter 5

Fateful Folly or Mothers Destiny? Mysteries of the Tynged

Thus far we have explored the complex issues surrounding the dynamics of the early part of the Fourth Branch; by taking a closer look at the children that are birthed by Aranrhod we can glean further wisdom. Having given some attention to Dylan we must now turn our gaze to the perplexing small thing that Aranrhod dropped from the folds of her womb.

The original Welsh text provides a stark and visceral description of the events that follow Dylan's birth, which again are lost in translation. After the birth and departure of Dylan and as Aranrhod drops the small thing, we are told that Gwydion –

> *"A chyn cael o neb guelet yr eil olwc arnaw, Gwydion a'y kymerth, ac a droes llen o bali yn y gylch, ac a'e cudyawd. Sef a cydyawd, y mwyn llawgist is traed y wely."*
> "And before anyone could get a second look at it, Gwydion took it and wrapped it in a sheet of brocaded silk and hid it. The place where he hid it was in a small chest at the foot of his bed."

The small thing or 'pethan' that Aranrhod drops is, in contrast to Dylan, unformed and to all intents and purposes a kind of afterbirth that bears no semblance to a human being, at least not yet. Gwydion wraps the small thing in a sheet of brocaded silk which may feel incidental, however, the appearance of brocaded silk is a common feature in the Four Branches of the Mabinogi. The fabric is deeply connected to ideas of sovereignty, transformation and magic. The wrapping of Lleu in brocaded silk not only hides the child but also prepares him for his future transformation into a hero, it is a conduit of magical transformation. The symbolism of the chest at the foot of Gwydion's bed is obvious as a secondary geostationary vessel that eventually leads to the birth of a fully formed child. One morning, Gwydion hears a cry from the chest, he opens it to find the folds of silk moving and the arms of a babe reaching through them. The original Welsh description is particularly visceral as it describes –

> *"Ac ual y hegyr, ef a weley uab bychan yn rwyuaw y ureicheu o blyc y llen ac yn y guascaru."*
> "As he opened it, he saw a small boy waving his arms free of the folds of the sheet and pushing it away."

The original language paints a visceral image of a child being birthed within the folds of the sheets parting as they would in a natural vaginal birth. The image the storyteller would have portrayed would have imitated a real birth.[47] The implication here is that Gwydion's chest has the magical capacity of acting as a secondary womb that contains all the necessary ingredients and prerequisites to gestate new life. A medieval audience would have been perplexed, bewildered and entertained by the concept of a man taking on the maternal role of not only gestating a child, but also choosing willingly to nurture and raise it. In time, Gwydion finds a wet-nurse in the local village to nourish the child who grows at an alarming rate, doubling his size in just over a year. This is not the first time that Gwydion crosses the gender divide that was the societal norm of medieval Wales. On several occasions Gwydion gives birth or facilitates the birthing of another being or nurtures them as a mother figure.

The first instance is that Gwydion as part of his punishment is transformed by Math into a sow and forced to breed with his brother and produce a piglet. Later in the Fourth Branch Gwydion has the instinct to follow a sow to find Lleu in the branches of the World Tree. Having taken on the *anian*, the essence of the sow, it would be reasonable to assume that Gwydion will forever have an association or an ability to connect empathically and telepathically with other sows. Perhaps a remnant of the nature of the sow remains a permanent aspect of his spirit, enabling him to connect to the animal in ways that other characters cannot. The second instance is perhaps more symbolic in his nurturing of the thing that Aranrhod drops, and whilst he does not physically birth the child, he certainly facilitates its gestation. The third example is the intentional birthing and fashioning of the magical bride to circumvent Aranrhod's fate that he facilitates with his uncle. In this example, two men are responsible for the creation of new life, something that would have perplexed and equally entertained the audience in its audacity.

We can consider Gwydion not only as a magician and trickster but as a transgressive individual who does not comply with social norms. These same qualities can be seen in the figure of Aranrhod who acts in a manner that betrays the maternal roles of the time. These transgressive behaviours are subtle and highly nuanced and will be explored fully later.

The events that follow form the crisis point that moves the remainder of the story forward. Gwydion takes the young boy who is as large as an eight-year-old, even though only four years have passed to meet his mother – Aranrhod. The place of meeting is Caer Aranrhod, the Fort of Arianrhod. This is highly unusual and particularly transgressive in that an unmarried woman would not have had her own domain or court, and a medieval audience would have understood the unusualness of this. She is the only woman in the entirety of the Mabinogi who has no obligatory bonds to a man, she is unmarried yet powerful. She seemingly does not recognise any social or kinship regulations which would have been normative at the time. Within her fort described in lush detail in the *Book of*

Taliesin she dwells apart, and perhaps in isolation from the societal and familiar norms around her. This divergence from the expected norms of womanhood further establishes Aranrhod as a liminal figure.

In the *Book of Taliesin,* we find this description of Aranrhod and her abode –

> *"Aranrot drem clot tra gwawr hinon, mwyhaf gwarth y marth, o parth brython, dybrys am y llys, efnys afon, afon a'e hechrys gwrys gwrth Terra. Gwenwyn y chynbyt kylchbyt eda."*
> "Aranrhod, her beauty exceeds the radiance of dawn, her shaming was the greatest shame for the Britons. A raging river rushes about her court, a savage river beats against the earth."[48]

The naming of Britons hints at collateral implications that affected the country at large, and whilst this idea is interesting, Haycock has suggested that the Brython component might be emended as *brithron* meaning wand and would thus neatly fit into the mythology.[49] If this is the case, that line would be translated as – "Her shaming came from stepping over the magic wand." In addition, these lines of poetry further corroborate the independent nature of Aranrhod as an individual who is not tied to any societal norms or to a man. Her home court, Caer Aranrhod in colloquial and vernacular lore lies out at sea approximately one mile offshore from the Iron Age hill fort of Dinas Dinlle (the fort of the city of Lleu) in the county of Arfon, only three miles west of the modern town of Caernarfon. Today it appears as a series of rocks visible only at low tide, but there may have been a time when it could have been reached on foot during the lowest of tides.

The placement of Caer Aranrhod out at sea in the vernacular tradition may be because of its watery nature within the poetry of the *Book of Taliesin*. The river that rages about her court suggests an island, the savage nature of the river beats relentlessly against the earth, and yet she is the axle, maintaining composure at its centre, whilst around her there may well be chaos. Upon her island, Aranrhod conducts the spinning of fates that turn around her, often merciful, at times savage and terrible.

Upon arriving at Caer Aranrhod, Gwydion and the unnamed child provoke her into placing three different *fates* upon the child. The discourse between Gwydion and Aranrhod and its tone is the reason why many scholars have considered Gwydion to be the father of Lleu. Their conversation which escalates to argument speaks of shame and embarrassment, which modern scholars have interpreted as the shame of incestual relations between herself and her brother, which as this book has demonstrated is an incorrect conclusion. Why then, does Aranrhod feel shame and embarrassment?

This likely stems from the narrative bleeding back into the customs of the apparent world, Aranrhod is no longer a virgin, yet she is unmarried, Gwydion serves to remind her of that fact and the social embarrassment that it causes. What is important to keep in mind when looking at these myths is that complex symbolic, magical, socio-political and societal values are interwoven into the tales. At times it is apparent that we are dealing with supernatural beings that stand outside of time and place, at other times we see the influence of social norms impeaching on the narrative, pulling us back into the apparent world. To see the mystery beneath we must at times un-weave the fabric of the narrative and look between the threads, as this book is intent on demonstrating. The driving force of this episode is not so much the shame that has been wrought upon Aranrhod, but how she responds to the child. From a mystical perspective for the child to be transformed and for order to be restored to the natural world, he must be pressed and pushed forward through the various trials and tribulations that lead to his ultimate transformation. Only Aranrhod has the power to instigate this.

Her response to Gwydion is to place three *tynged* on the child; in doing so she demonstrates the immense power that she has over the fate and destiny of the young boy. To understand the significance and impact of the three tynged, we must look to the meaning of the word within the Welsh language.

A simple Welsh-English translation results in the meaning of tynged being interpreted as 'destiny, doom, fate'. This oversimplifies the term and it loses its nuance, the meaning of tynged implies not only that which has been pre-destined, but also that which by an unknown force has been appointed beforehand and pre-determined. A tynged results in an unavoidable course of events that cannot be easily circumvented. In addition, and figuratively the word can be interpreted as prophecy, to predict, fate, or destiny by act of magic. Evidently Aranrhod has magical abilities, and her capabilities are fiercely demonstrated.

The careful use of the term tynged is attempting to reveal a hidden meaning, and it is precisely that hidden meaning that the polytheist and mythologist strives to uncover. In the First Branch of the Mabinogi, the primary protagonist Pwyll states that the peculiar events he and his retinue witness during their initial encounter with Rhiannon contains an 'ystyr hud', a magical meaning, which offers a clue to the quester to notice and take heed of these occurrences. When we stop and pay attention to them, we can sense the influence of the supernatural and otherworldly forces breaking through the surface of the narrative. The tynged is an example of this as were the pigs that I explored earlier.

Aranrhod places three tynged upon the child

The first is that he shall not be given a name unless it is given by her. Secondly, he shall not bear arms unless given by her, and thirdly, he shall not marry a woman who is currently of the race of the earth. Gwydion circumvents the first two tynged by magical means and succeeds in breaking the tynged and forces Aranrhod to name the child and give him arms. The name that she gives the child is Lleu Llaw Gyffess meaning 'light one, he of skilful hand', after he skilfully strikes a wren's leg with a stone between the tendon and the bone. Further magical meaning occurs at this precise moment, the wren in British folklore is associated with the role of the sacred King and is often referred to as the King of birds, albeit it is the smallest of British birds. The wounding of the wren foreshadows his own wounding that ultimately leads to his transformation. In Welsh myths, Kings are often wounded in their legs or feet, such as Brân in the Second Branch of the Mabinogi. This peculiar episode is foretelling the events of Lleu and his rise to sovereignty.

Another magical disguise by Gwydion tricks Aranrhod into believing that her fort is under attack, she arms the magically disguised boy and thus the second tynged is broken. When a woman cannot be found of a race that is currently on the face of the earth, a queer turn of phrase that implies that other races may well indeed exist, or had existed in the past, Gwydion turns to his uncle to break it. It may appear on the surface of things that they succeeded in doing that, but they fail. The maiden they create who is initially named Blodeu(w)edd – meaning of flowers, betrays Lleu and is turned into the first owl to exist and is then named Blodeu(w)edd – meaning, flower face an old Welsh term for owl.

If we look for an *'ystyr hud'*, a magical meaning in all this what wisdom can we find? Each tynged can be interpreted in ways that provide profound insights for those on a path of personal transformation or initiation, which is essentially what the Fourth Branch is expressing and attempting to teach. It does so in surprisingly modern ways, myth after all does exist in the moment. Not only does it express profound spiritual illumination, but it can also be seen as a metaphor for the damage we have caused the earth and offer a way by which we can fix it. If we take a closer look at the three tynged we can deduce further wisdoms.

"He shall not be given a name unless given by me."

Social Implications: In medieval Welsh culture, receiving a name from a person of high status or parental lineage signified legitimacy and social recognition. By not having a name, the child cannot be fully incorporated into society or into any meaningful relationship, either with Aranrhod or anyone else. This essentially leaves the child in a liminal state where they do not belong anywhere or to anyone. Gwydion is unable to name the child, but Aranrhod can, reiterating that she is the rightful parent whereas Gwydion is not.

Mystical Interpretation: The act of naming someone or something as we have seen in the episode between Math and Dylan leads to a transformation of identity and emulates the true nature of the individual or thing. The process of receiving a name is symbolic of the transformation of the self. For an initiate, this can be seen as the shedding of the old identity and the emergence of a new and true self, and this is precisely the journey that we see on the stage of the Fourth Branch. Initiatory traditions will invariably encourage or place a new name upon the initiate, and contemporary western paganism is replete with individuals who have adopted a name that more accurately reflects their true self. The name given by Aranrhod can be interpreted as a divine or spiritual recognition of one's true nature or purpose. The name given to the child is Lleu, meaning light; Llaw Gyffes, meaning of skilful hand. Whilst Lleu can and is used in Welsh culture as a personal noun, it is its adjective form that is of interest here – light, brightness and that which is bright.

From a mystical perspective, if Dylan represents the unformed and undifferentiated consciousness, then Lleu represents the formative principle that has expression in the world – light, the inner brightness of the initiate. By their own inherent skills, the initiate develops the light of self, which is shone out into the world, inspiring, influencing, attempting to restore the order that has been disrupted. This tynged involves a deep recognition and acceptance of one's true essence or anian, to know oneself. It implies that identity is not self-proclaimed but must be discovered and conferred through a higher, perhaps divine, process where the individual gifts of the initiate are revealed. And in that revealing the medicine that each of us are intended to bring into the world to restore order is brought to light. This transforms the initiate into a co-creator with the forces around them, rather than a figure that takes advantage.

"He shall not bear arms unless given by me."

Social Implications: Authority and power in medieval Welsh society were primary driving forces, the right to bear arms was linked to status, responsibility, and the authority to protect and lead. Aranrhod's tynged denies Lleu the tools necessary to serve as a protector of the land and its people, consequently preventing him from gaining fame as a great warrior.[50] As the son of Math the high King, Lleu's inability to bear arms would render him socially impotent.

Mystical Interpretation: Bearing arms can be seen as a metaphor for assuming one's power and responsibilities and identifying the skills that the name Lleu Llaw Gyffes pertain to. Not only is the initiate filled with a preternatural light, but they also have inherent skills that shines that light into the apparent world. Discovering the nature of these skills is arming the initiate with the tools required to not only transform themselves, but their realm of influence. This tynged indicates that true power and authority must be conferred through the guidance of higher wisdom or divine inspiration. It suggests that the initiate must undergo a period of preparation and prove their worthiness before being granted the tools or more abstractly, the power necessary for their journey. The wielding of power is a double-edged sword, we can use it proactively to bring about immense transformation, or we can turn it on ourselves or others. Spiritual strength and wisdom are required for the initiate to wield their tools or their arms in a manner that is in accordance with their inner light. This tynged can also be seen as a test of inner strength and spiritual maturity, and it implies that the initiate must develop inner virtues and strength before they can be entrusted with external power.

"He shall not marry a woman who is currently of the race of the earth."

Social Implications: Marriage in medieval Welsh culture was not only a personal union but also a means of forming alliances and consolidating power. Marriage ensured continuation by the providing of an heir that would inherit the legacy of their parents. It brought stability to situations where tensions might prevail. Without a wife and an heir, the legacy of Lleu as the only male child of Math comes to an end, thus the tynged threatens the entire stability of the Kingdom of Gwynedd.

Mystical Interpretation: This tynged is multifaceted in its possible meanings. The words chosen are peculiar, a woman that is currently not of the race of the earth. What can Aranrhod have meant by those words? These carefully chosen words imply that other races might once have existed or co-existed with humans, it accommodates that other races may yet arrive to inhabit the earth, or it might be a reference to the Tylwyth Teg (the fair folk) of Welsh tradition, in that they may well have lived among us at one point in time. A general internet search with the name Blodeu(w)edd will result in countless hits where she is described as a 'fairy bride', yet there is little evidence within the myths to suggest that she is of the race of the Tylwyth Teg.

Blodeu(w)edd is a creature made entirely from flowers and then imbued with sentiency by the magic of Math and Gwydion, or so they believe. Instead, she demonstrates a consciousness that is entirely her own, she does not conform to the standards or obligations placed upon her. She is the wild, untamed aspect of nature. In many ways she is like Aranrhod in that she stands outside of social norms and familial structures, she actively rejects the obligations that humans impose upon her. This tynged was destined to fail, man cannot tame nature. The creation of Blodeu(w)edd is another example of the natural order being disrupted and of the arrogance of mankind in believing he can control the forces of nature.

This tynged can be interpreted as a call for a union beyond the physical and mundane that is based on integrity, symbiosis and honour. This can be understood as an allegory for the sacred marriage, or '*hieros gamos,*' where the soul seeks union with the divine or higher consciousness, in this case that union should be through the powers of nature. The tynged questions what the initiate is betrothed to, what is it that binds them to concepts or desires that may not be beneficial or potentially transformative. The flower maiden who was created to be a passive partner to Lleu transforms into an expression of independent, uncontrolled will, her first conscious act is that of adultery, she is driven by what she feels rather than the obligations placed upon her. She is the unadulterated force of nature in all its raw glory and power, she is the animistic, divine force in nature. Eventually she is transformed into a creature that can only inhabit the nighttime, an interesting parallel that she becomes the dark to Lleu's light.

The three tynged placed upon Lleu Llaw Gyffes can be seen as stages in the journey of spiritual initiation and transformation. They symbolize:

1. *Discovery of the true self:* Recognizing and embracing one's identity beyond societal labels and ego, finding the light that is the true expression of who you are.
2. *Preparation and Empowerment:* Developing the inner strength, virtues, and readiness to wield power and responsibility in a manner that is sagacious and transformative.
3. *Union with the Divine:* Transcending personal limitations and desires to seek a deeper, spiritual connection with the divine or animistic forces of nature.

It is difficult to interpret the genealogy of Bonedd yr Arwyr to determine if the language is suggesting that Arianrhod is the mother of Lleu, Dylan and Blodeu(w)edd. Whilst there are symbolic similarities between Aranrhod and Blodeu(w)edd, and the genealogy might well be hinting at a subtle connection between the two, it is inconclusive. One might argue that the creation of the flower maiden is as a direct consequence of the tynged that is placed upon Lleu, at a stretch we might consider this a catalyst for the birthing of Blodeu(w)edd. At times, themes and characters in the Mabinogi may overlap in complex ways. Aranrhod and Blodeu(w)edd might well be connected through broader mythological themes of fertility, sovereignty and magical creation, but the question of actual parenthood in relation to Aranrhod is subject to personal interpretation.

To summarise the roles of the offspring of Math and those of Aranrhod we may consider them to embody the following qualities –

- *Dylan:*

The Formless Principle
Undifferentiated Consciousness
Passivity
Quiddity
The Unconscious or Eternal Self

- *Lleu Llaw Gyffes:*

The Formative Principle
Active Will
The apparent personality
Skills
The Conscious or Apparent Self

- *Blodeu(w)edd*

The Manifesting Principle
Animistic Force of Nature
The Wild and Untamed
Divinity of the Natural World
The Collective Consciousness

As immanent forces within the initiate, the living landscape of myth bursts into life when we place ourselves in the position of these mythical characters. The implementation of this change of perspective then places us in direct relationship with Aranrhod who becomes the axle of that experience. From a mythical perspective, Dylan and Lleu are twins, two sides of the same coin, formed and created by the union of Math the King, with the goddess of the land. The creation of the children is an attempt by the King to restore the order that Gwydion and

Gilfaethwy disrupted and can be seen as a powerful metaphor of initiation for the modern polytheist.

One half of the initiate is of the nature of the sea itself, a component of which will eternally reside in the undifferentiated consciousness of the ocean. This is a powerful metaphor for the nature of the human spirit, that we are inseparable from the oneness of the ocean, from the great mother herself. This aspect is held beautifully in the metaphor of Dylan, not only is Dylan the sea and the deep simultaneously but has its expression in wave, hence the name Dylan Eil Ton. There is a profound mystery that can be derived from this name alone. A wave is something that the entire sea or ocean is doing, it is not observing it passively or separate from it, it is an active component of the sea that is given shape and form for only a brief amount of time. To delve deeper into the mystery beyond the ninth wave, you as an expression of Dylan are something that the universe is doing right now, you are not being observed or watched from afar, you are a component of the universe expressing itself. It is to this mystery that Dylan alludes.

Lleu, the once nameless child, cursed by his mother to not have a name, arms or a consort of the race of the earth embodies the qualities of light, illumination and skill that you contain. Aranrhod is the catalyst and harbinger of twins that serve to rectify and bring about a balanced state of the world. The tynged are not curses, they are driving forces that compel the initiate onwards and forwards towards profound transformation. And at the centre of that she stands, the still point around which the wheels of initiation and transformation spin.

Chapter 6

Weaving the Threads of Gender and Ecology

Your magic weaves a tapestry of old,
A web of wisdom and stories untold.
A world where harmony reigned supreme,
Where mankind slept in earth's sweet dream.

Man awoke to humanity's din,
And forgot to listen to the voice within,
The whispers of earth, an ancient pain,
The cries of suffering, wounds that remain.

Your secrets echo through ancient trees,
A call to awaken, to hear Goewin's pleas,
To dry her tears, and step into our light,
To change from within, with power and might.

Gender is a pressing issue in modernity, and yet it's significance in the past would not have gone unnoticed, albeit for different reasons. In contrast to the 21st Century, medieval Wales was a highly gendered society in which gender roles were understood and fit neatly into boxes of conformity. Gwydion and Aranrhod in the Fourth Branch of the Mabinogi exhibit behaviours and characteristics that challenged these traditional gender roles and identity, which can be analysed to derive several layers of meaning. When we approach the myths, it can be a challenge to navigate and circumvent what might appear to be strict gendered roles. However, my hope is that this book has demonstrated that whilst figures like Dylan and Lleu are gendered for the purposes of narration and storytelling, the meaning of their names transcend gender. We all contain the essence of Dylan and the potential of Lleu within us regardless of our gender identity. Blodeu(w)edd can be perceived as the wild and untamed nature of nature that is an inexorable aspect of you.

Parentage can also be problematic, particularly for those of us who will never experience that as an aspect of our lives. And whilst the paternity of the children demonstrates a relationship between different forces within the narrative, it is evident that it is maternity that is of importance within the text.[51] Characters are primarily named after their mothers, examples are Gwydion son of Dôn, Aranrhod daughter of Dôn, Math son of Mathonwy,[52] the three sons of wicked Gilfaethwy (who was a mother twice).

Although expressed as a male character within the narrative, Gwydion exhibits traits that transcend conventional masculine roles. He is a powerful magician and a manipulator, using cunning and subterfuge rather than brute strength to achieve his ends whilst simultaneously displaying a gentle and loving component to his personality. This blend of traditionally masculine and feminine attributes may stem from the fact that Gwydion lived as a female animal and thus has the capacity to cross the gender divide.

Aranrhod's refusal to conform to maternal expectations and her defiance against male authority figures, interestingly positions her as a transgressive figure. She challenges the traditional role of women as nurturing mothers and compliant sisters, asserting her autonomy and control over her own domain and destiny.

The transformations that Gwydion facilitates, from Lleu in his upbringing and transformation from eagle to human, the fashioning of Blodeu(w)edd, to the various disguises and magical interventions that he creates, emphasise the theme of fluid identity. In the Welsh language the shape and form of something or someone, it's *'rhith'* is not necessarily stable and concrete, it can be changed by the will of a magician, it is essentially an illusion or a disguise, something that we wear. This idea of fluid identity and gender is commonplace in the 21st century but would have been transgressive and challenging in medieval Wales. Aranrhod and Gwydion challenge fixed notions of self and suggest that identity is mutable and constructed rather than innate, rigid or immovable. By transgressing gender roles, Gwydion and Arianrhod subvert traditional mythical archetypes, prompting a revaluation of cultural narratives about gender and power. Their actions reveal the limitations and contradictions inherent in rigid gender binaries and invite a more nuanced understanding of human behaviour and identity. This idiosyncrasy of myth and its applicability to modernity is testament to the timeless nature of myth.

In addition, Gwydion and Aranrhod are deeply connected to magic and their magical abilities allow them to navigate and manipulate the world in ways that defy traditional gender constraints. This highlights the liberating potential of the supernatural to subvert societal norms and throughout the Fourth Branch we can clearly see the interplay of these forces.

In response to the defilement of Goewin, the natural order of the world has been disrupted, as King and sovereign it is Math's responsibility to bring about balance. The antagonists in the tale are Gwydion and Gilfaethwy, following their punishment Gwydion strives to help his uncle restore balance and order. As previously explored, Gwydion and Gilfaethwy can be seen as the corruption within the human condition that has led to the ongoing defilement of the earth and her resources, embodied in the myth by Goewin, the once loving face of the goddess. The vengeful or terrible mother arises in the guise of Aranrhod as the transformer of destiny and fate, the turner of wheels who strives to bring about balance. This is a message that is particularly pertinent to the 21st century considering the current climate crisis. The myth attempts to rectify this by birthing a child that is balanced and in symbiotic relationship with the earth.

The environmental crisis we face today parallels the themes of initiation, transformation, and renewal found in the Fourth Branch of the Mabinogi. While it may seem daunting, and sometimes feels like we have run out of time, there are still many steps we can take to repair the damage we have done to the earth, to Goewin.

Assuming the roles of Dylan and Lleu as the formless and formative principles within ourselves, and working in balance with the qualities of Blodeu(w)edd as a representation of the manifesting principle, there is much we can do to transform the world we live in. In doing so we serve to repair the damage done by the defilement of Goewin. Personal transformation leads to accepting responsibility for our actions and having the ability to respond to those actions in a manner that strives to rectify them. As individuals and members of wider communities we all have the power to inspire collective action. This does not need to be grand or massive, simply attending a local beach clean-up, or organising one yourself is immensely empowering and beneficial. When we act locally, we inspire globally.

For some advocacy and activism are the way forward whereas others might be drawn towards education and outreach. Consider the landscape that you live in, your square mile and whether there are plans or projects of restoration and conservation that could do with your help or attention. Encourage sustainable agriculture and food systems by doing what you can to purchase locally and to support sustainable farming. Our actions can have enormous impact, even if our realm of influence is locality specific.

While the task of repairing the earth is immense, it is crucial to maintain hope and perseverance. Personal transformation, as symbolized by Dylan and Lleu in the Mabinogi, can lead to broader collective change. Every action counts, and collective efforts can create significant impact. It is not too late if we remain committed to making positive changes. By taking these steps and embodying the transformative spirit of the Mabinogi heroes, we can work towards healing the earth in the guise of Goewin and foster a sustainable future for generations to come.

Chapter 7

Ways to Connect with Arianrhod

Wyt Harddwch,
Wyt Urddas,
Rho i'm Aranrhod,
Dy 'ras.

You are beauty,
You are dignity,
Bestow upon me,
O Arianrhod,
Your grace.

Symbols are useful for allowing us to connect on a subtle level to the virtues and attributes of Arianrhod. They can be utilised as devotional focal points, to create altars and shrines in her honour. By carrying her sacred symbols about our person, we can be reminded daily about her virtues and influence in our lives.

Symbols

The Starry Wheel:

This reminds us of the turning of celestial bodies around us and of Aranrhod's position at their centre, where she observes and witnesses the wheels of life and the universe turning around her. Use it to connect to the cosmos, to the great forces around you. When the cosmos or situations in your life feel like they are running ahead or despite of you, consider the still point at the centre and mediate on it to bring you back into balance with the wheel.

(Starry Wheel)

The Triskele:
This much-loved ancient symbol captures the role of Aranrhod as the sacred garan. Consider the spinning arms of the triskele as the three aspects of self as expressed by Dylan, Lleu and Blodeu(w)edd: the Children of Math. By focusing on the centre point where all three arms originate, we can pull our attention towards Aranrhod and direct our focus towards the axle that maintains the turning of these aspects of self.

(Triskele)

The Spindle:
This symbol captures the energy of Arianrhod as the goddess who weaves the subtle aspects of our lives, the threads of which might not be obvious or apparent. In contrast to her role as the garan, this is an active symbol that can help us connect with the various threads of our lives. Use it to meditate upon the various

components of your life that you would like Arianrhod's guidance with.

Spindle

Silver Coins:

Silver coins of any denomination or currency are useful items to place as offerings for Arianrhod. If you are thus inclined and have the skills, create your own silvery coins in honour of the goddess and carry them about your person, such items can be carved with the other symbols that are pertinent to her.

White/Silver plants and flowers:

Use plants that are silvery white in part or totality to give as offerings to Arianrhod. In the authors experience, Mugwort whose undersides are silver are particularly loved by her. Sea Holly and Lambs Ears (Stachys Byzantina) are also useful as offerings and decorative plants for a sacred space. Use the plant as a nosegay; a small bouquet to offer on altars or shrines. Or create incenses or oils to honour her and to gift as offerings.

The Tower:

An image of a tower, particularly potent if depicted upon an island, drawn or sourced from an artist or other outlet is a powerful symbol to connect to the liminal quality of Arianrhod. The author uses The Tower card from a popular tarot deck to act as a proxy Caer Arianrhod upon an altar. Liminality is a powerful state which can assist us to connect not only with the goddess but to the virtues that she embodies.

The Cauldron:

Whilst this symbol is not an obvious choice for Arianrhod, it is a powerful metaphor for her womb which births Dylan and Lleu and for the holding quality of the axle. She holds the experience of the three divisions of self in her womb, within a cauldron of potential manifestation. Loved by the Celts, the cauldron is often a catch all symbol for the qualities embodied by several deities, spirits and concepts.

Creating a space designated for the honouring and veneration of Arianrhod can take any shape or form that works for you. The author uses a shelf on a bookcase that holds a statue of Arianrhod in the centre, candles adorn the space as do several of the items listed above. A small metal cauldron sits before the statue and is used to burn offerings of poetry to the goddess, these poems are written on slivers of parchment, read out to her over the course of a week and then burnt on a Monday evening in her honour. The same cauldron doubles as a burning vessel to offer incense.

Arianrhod Incense

Any of the following ingredients can be substituted for natural materials that capture the same qualities as those listed.

In a pestle and mortar or cauldron blend together –

- 1 part Pine resin or Copal resin.
- ½ part dried Mugwort
- ½ part crushed Juniper berries
- ¼ part dried Wormwood

- ¼ part dried Vervain
- ¼ part Lavender or few drops of Lavender essential oil
- A pinch of yarrow
- A sprinkling of pine needles
- Add a few drops of Mugwort and Rosemary essential oil to slightly moisten the mixture. Place in an amber coloured jar and position to bake on a sunny windowsill for one month before use. Depending on amount of oil used you may need to break the mixture up with a knife before using. Burn the incense on charcoal briquettes designed for incense or Shisha smoking.

To create an offering or anointing oil of this incense, place the raw ingredients in a high-grade oil of your choosing and simmer gently for 24 hours in a crock-pot or slow cooker. Strain the oil from the raw materials and bottle in amber glass.

Saining Bundle

Gather fresh stems of Mugwort, Lavender, Rosemary and Wormwood. Position them in a bundle no longer than 8 inches long to maintain their structural integrity. Use elastic bands to hold the top and bottom of the bundle, with natural string or cotton thread begin to wrap the bundle tightly from one end to the other. When tightly bound, tie off the ends and hang the bundle to dry. Remove the elastic bands before setting fire to the bundle, blow out the flames and waft the bundle to disperse the fragrant smoke.

Aligning Oneself with the Virtues of Arianrhod

Aranrhod's role as the sacred axle, the garan, or the still point at the centre of the turning wheel can offer profound spiritual wisdom that can be applied to various aspects of life and spiritual practice. Here are some key insights we can glean from her symbolic significance:

Being the Garan – Balance and Cantering:

Aranrhod teaches the importance of maintaining inner stability and composure amidst the constant changes and cycles of life. Just as the axle is the still point that ensures the wheels spin smoothly, finding your own centre allows you to navigate life's ups and downs with grace and balance. Emulate Aranrhod's virtues in your everyday life and social circles by being the 'garan' that your communities and the world needs. Being the garan requires that one is engaged in practices that help ground you, such as meditation, mindfulness, pathworking. These practices can help you find your own still point and maintain equilibrium within your own life, and inspired others to find their own garan.

Connection to the Cosmos:

In her guise as the turner of wheels, Arianrhod's position as the centre of the wheel highlights the interconnectedness of all things. Just as the spokes of a wheel connect to the central axle, everything in the universe is interconnected, and we are all part of a larger whole. This mystery is held in the teachings and virtues of Arianrhod.

Cultivate an awareness of your place in the cosmos and reflect on how your actions, thoughts, and energy contribute to the larger web of life, nothing is separate, all is connected.

Cycles and Continuity:

Embrace the natural cycles of life, birth, growth, death, and rebirth. Arianrhod's association with the wheel reminds us that life is cyclical, and each phase is necessary for growth and transformation. Take note and heed of these cycles in your own life. If inclined, offer yourself as a facilitator of rituals that help others to mark these passages in their own lives. Learn to flow with the changes and transitions in life rather than resisting them. Recognize that each cycle brings new opportunities for learning and growth.

Sacred Feminine Energy:
Embrace the sacred feminine power that Arianrhod embodies, which is often associated with intuition and creative potential. She embodies the fierce qualities of the mother who knows what is best for her children. Embrace these aspects of yourself and honour the feminine energy within and around you. Allow your creative energies to flow and to identify and nurture the creative endeavours and skills of others around you. Whether through art, music, writing, or other forms of expression, tap into your inner creativity to connect with Arianrhod's energy.

The Immanency of the Tynged in your Life

Use this technique to identify the qualities of the three tynged in your life. To achieve this, you will need an oracle of your choosing. A deck of tarot cards, and oracle deck, runes, ogham, whichever tool sings to you. From this tool randomly select three cards/items and place them facedown or unrevealed before you in this pattern –

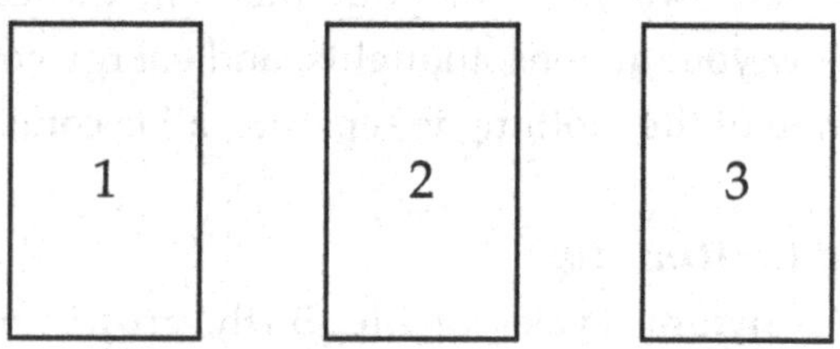

Bring to mind an image of a tower upon an island, with waves crashing around it, this is the liminal home of Arianrhod, a place from where you can call her for clarity or assistance. As you do repeat the following words or similar, which can be used as a general invocation or a song of praise to Arianrhod at any time and for any exercise.

"Wyt harddwch, wyt Urddas, rho i'm Arianrhod dy 'ras."[53]

"You are beauty, you are dignity, bestow upon me, O Arianrhod, Your grace."

- Consider the first card/item and ask, 'What is my name?' i.e. the identity that you carry in this life. An identity that is a fusion of your own input and creation and the influences around you. Who are you?
- Consider the second card and ask, 'What are my arms?', what are the skills that you have that best serve yourself, your communities and the earth? What is the medicine that you have to offer the world in reparation of Goewin?
- Reveal the final card/item and ask, 'To what am I betrothed?'. Consider this question as the things in your life that tie you to other things, people or principles. These can be positive, negative or neutral in nature. Which are useful, and which ones no longer serve you or denigrate you?

Conclusion

As this short journey with Arianrhod concludes it is my hope that it will initiate not only a profound personal relationship between yourself and the goddess, but one that will lead to deep transformation. The limited scope of this book could not hope to cover every aspect of this multifaceted and complex goddess, nor every single detail that sings from her expression. Instead, it acts as a door through which you might intensify your studies and experience of her. There is more to discover about the once elusive Arianrhod, she is there at the centre of all things, just waiting for you to approach. Therefore, find the stillness within your – your garan – for it is in that stillness that she can be found.

May her beauty, grace and fierceness enrich and bring to your spiritual endeavours light, direction and clarity.

A Guide to Welsh Pronunciation

A glossary of words can be found at the authors YouTube page – https://www.youtube.com/channel/UCtpV2UP46Avd76h7OSWY4Lw

The stress of any word almost exclusively stands on the penultimate syllable. A vowel is elongated if it appears with a circumflex above it. For example – Don without the circumflex would be pronounced as *Donn*. With the addition of a circumflex – Dôn – would be pronounced *Dawn*.

The Welsh alphabet

a, b, c, ch, d, dd, e, f, ff, g, ng, h, i, l, ll, m, n, o, p, ph, r, rh, s, t, th, u, w, y

Welsh Vowels

a-	Short as in 'mat'	long as in 'farmer'
e-	Short as in 'let'	long as in 'bear'
i-	Short as in 'pit'	long as in 'meet'
o-	Short as in 'lot'	long as in 'lore'
u-	Short as in 'ill'	long as in 'limb'
w-	Short as in 'look'	long as in 'fool'
y-	Short as in 'up'	long as in 'under'

Welsh Consonants

Some may be similar in sound to their English counterparts but with emphasis on heavy aspiration of sound.

b-	as in 'bin'
c-	as in 'cat'
ch-	guttural as in 'loch', never as in 'chin'
d-	as in 'dad'
dd-	as in 'th' sound in 'them' never as in 'thin'
e-	as in 'elephant'

f-	as in 'van'
ff-	as in 'off'
g-	as in 'gate' never as in 'gem'
ng-	as in 'song' never as in 'linger'
h-	as in 'hit', it is never silent
l-	as in 'lit'
ll-	no counterpart, voice by placing tip of tongue in 'L' position and exhaling voicelessly through the sides of the mouth.
m-	as in 'mat'
n-	as in 'nit'
p-	as in 'part'
ph-	as in 'phrase'
r-	is trilled by the tip of the tongue as 'ravioli' in Italian
rh-	no counterpart, voice by placing tongue in 'r' position and exhale quickly and harshly but voicelessly, through the narrow gap the lips form.
s-	as in 'sit' never as in 'kiss'
t-	as in 'tap'
th-	as in 'thick' never as in 'them'

Endnotes

1. Dôn appears as a mother-type deity, or an over-deity in the Fourth Branch of the Mabinogi. In modern Welsh Polytheism she is often compared to a earth-type divinity and particularly associated with rivers.
2. Davies, Sioned. The Mabinogion. P242.
3. Ifans & Ifans. Y Mabinogion. P 55.
4. Williams, Mark. The Celtic Myths that Shape the Way we Think. Pp 206-211.
5. Ford, Patrick K. Math Uab Mathonwy. P xviii. Whilst seemingly different in spelling the same sound applies to the Middle Welsh designation 'Aranrot' and the Modern Welsh version 'Aranrhod'.
6. The letter 'y' in this version of her name is pronounced as 'ee'.
7. Bromwich, Rachel, Trioedd Ynys Prydein (TYP). P284.
8. ibid. P284.
9. Williams, Sir Ifor, Pedeir Keinc y Mabinogi – University of Wales Press (UWP), 1930. Pages 269-270.
10. Translation by Kristoffer Hughes.
11. https://www.geiriadur.ac.uk
12. Graves, Robert. The White Goddess. P 98.
13. https://mabinogionastronomy.blogspot.com/2014/09/don-and-aranrhod.html
14. Bromwich, TYP, UWP. Page 284.
15. Bromwich, Rachel. TYP. P 81.
16. Bromwich. TYP. P 284.
17. Bromwich, TYP. P 185.
18. Bromwich, TYP. P 208.
19. Together with 24 other medieval manuscripts, compiled into a genealogical collection called 'Bonedd yr Arwyr' by P.C. Bartrum.
20. For deeper discourse see, Hughes, Kristoffer. Cerridwen: Celtic Goddess of Inspiration. P 29-52.

21. Morus-Baird, Gwilym. Taliesin Origins. P 58-60.
22. Thomas, Gwyn. Y Traddodiad Barddol. P 13.
23. Olding, Frank. The Taliesin Sourcebook. P 183.
24. Williams, Ifor. Pedeir Keinc y Mabinogi. P 69.
25. Translated by the author.
26. Thomas, Bevan, Donovan (eds). Geiriadur Prifysgol Cymru. P 685.
27. Pleural of Cyfarwydd.
28. Davies, Sioned, Y Mabinogion. ix.
29. Williams, Ifor. Sir. PKM. P 27.
30. Ford, Patrick K. The Mabinogi. P3.
31. Parker. The Four Branches of the Mabinogi. P 653.
32. Roberts, Brynley F. Rhagymadrodd i Y Mabinogion gan, Dafydd & Rhianon Ifans. P xiii.
33. Davies, Sioned. The Mabinogion. P xxv.
34. My translation of Williams, Ifor. Pedeir Keinc y Mabinogi. P xxiii.
35. The flower maiden appears with two distinct names, Blodeuedd (of flowers) and Bloeuwedd (flower face). Throughout this text her name will appear as Blodeu(w)edd to include both versions.
36. Ford. Math fab Mathonwy. P xvi.
37. Williams. Pedeir Keinc y Mabinogi. P 67.
38. Dictionary of the Welsh Language.
39. Jenkins, Dafydd. The Law of Hywel Dda. P33.
40. Carey, John. A British Myth of Origins. P 31.
41. Sheehan, Sarah. Matrilinear subjects, ambiguity, bodies and metamorphoses in the Fourth Branch of the Mabinogi. P 325.
42. Williams, Ifor. Pedeir Keinc y Mabinogi. P 150-151
43. Ziser, Sarah. Performing a Literary Paternity Test. P 203.
44. Arfon, meaning near or facing Môn, modern day Ynys Môn (isle of Anglesey), and is a county in the Kingdom of Gwynedd.

45. Bartrum, P.C. Early Welsh Genealogical Tracts. The orthography has been modernized by Bartrum.
46. Haycock, Marged. LPBOT. Original Welsh, P 182. English translation by Kristoffer Hughes.
47. Valente, Roberta, L. Gwydion & Aranrhod, crossing the borders of gender in Math, in The Mabinogi: A book of essays. P 339.
48. Hughes, Kristoffer. Cerridwen. P 73-74.
49. Haycock. LPBOT. P 326.
50. Valente. Mabinogi Essays. P 341.
51. Sheehan, Sarah. Matrilinear subjects, ambiguity, bodies and metamorphoses in the Fourth Branch of the Mabinogi. P 331-336.
52. Bromwich suggested that Mathonwy may well be a matronymic. TYP. P 438.
53. Visit the authors YouTube page @ Kristoffer Hughes, for a video demonstrating the correct pronunciation of this verse.

Bibliography

Primary sources:

The White Book of Rhydderch (Llyfr Gwyn Rhydderch), Peniarth Manuscript 4, National Library of Wales.

https://www.library.wales/discover-learn/digital-exhibitions/manuscripts/the-middle-ages/white-book-of-rhydderch

The Book of Taliesin (Llyfr Taliesin), Peniarth Manuscript 2, National Library of Wales.

https://www.library.wales/discover-learn/digital-exhibitions/manuscripts/the-middle-ages/book-of-taliesin

Peniarth Manuscript 131, National Library of Wales.

https://viewer.library.wales/6057827#?xywh=-1382%2C-1%2C5979%2C5020&cv=21

Secondary Sources:

Bartrum, P.C. (1966). *Early Welsh Genealogical Tracts*. Cardiff: Wales U.P.

Boyd, M. (2017). *Four Branches of the Mabinogi*. Broadview Press Ltd.

Breeze, Andrew. (2009). *The origins of the Four branches of the Mabinogi*. Leominster: Gracewing.

Bromwich, Rachel. (2014). *Trioedd Ynys Prydein*. University of Wales Press.

Brown, M. and Williams, E. (2022). *The Mab*. Unbound Publishing.

Carey, John. (1991). A British Myth of Origins? *History of Religions*, 31(1), pp.24–38. doi:https://doi.org/10.1086/463254.

Conley, K., Harvard Celtic Colloquium and Harvard University Department of Celtic Languages and Literatures (2011). *Proceedings of the Harvard Celtic Colloquium: volume XXVIII, 2008*. Cambridge, Mass.; London Harvard Univ. Press.

Conran, Tony. (1992). *Welsh Verse*. Seren Books.

Davies, Sioned. (1993). *Pedeir Keinc Y Mabinogi*. Gomer Press.

Davies, Sioned. (2018). *Mabinogion.* Oxford University Press.

Ford, P.K. (1992). *Ystoria Taliesin*. University of Wales press.

Ford, P.K. (1999). *Math Uab Mathonwy*. Ford & Bailie Pub.

Ford, P.K. (2019). *The Mabinogi and other Medieval Welsh tales.* : Oakland, California: University of California Press.

Graves, Robert. and Lindop, G. (2013). *The white goddess: a historical grammar of poetic myth.* New York: Farrar, Straus and Giroux.

Greenfield, Trevor. (ed) (2014). *Naming the Goddess*. John Hunt Publishing.

Gruffydd, W.J. (2013). *Folklore and Myth in the Mabinogion – A Lecture Delivered at the National Museum of Wales on 27 October 1950*. Wakeman Press.

Gruffydd, William John. (1928). *Math Vab Mathonwy*. university of Wales press.

Guest, Charlotte. (1937). *The Mabinogion;* London, J.M. Dent & Co.; New York, E.P. Dutton & Co. Reprint.

Haycock, Marged. (2015). *Legendary poems from the Book of Taliesin*. Aberystwyth: Cmcs Publications.

Hughes, Kristoffer. (2021). *Cerridwen*. Llewellyn Worldwide.

Ifans, Dafydd, Ifans, Rhiannon. and Roberts, B.F. (2007). *Y Mabinogion: diweddariad*. Llandysul: Gomer.

Ifans, Rhiannon. (1999). *Gwerthfawrogi'r chwedlau*. university of Wales press.

Jenkins, Dafydd. (2000). *The Law of Hywel Dda: law texts from medieval Wales*. Llandysul: Gomer.

Jones, G. and Jones, T. (2000). *The Mabinogion*. London: Everyman.

Lewis, G. and Williams, R. (2019). *The Book of Taliesin: poems of warfare and praise in an enchanted Britain*. London, England; New York, New York, USA: Penguin Classics.

Lewys Môn (1975). *Gwaith Lewys Môn*. Gwasg Prifysgol Cymru.

Lyle, E. (2018). *Celtic Myth in the 21st Century*. University of Wales Press.

Morus-Baird, Gwilym. (2023). *Taliesin Origins*. Celtic Source.

Nagy, Joseph Falaky, Jones, L. and Ford, P.K. (2005). *Heroic poets and poetic heroes in Celtic tradition: a festschrift for Patrick K. Ford*. Dublin, Ireland; Portland, Or: Four Courts Press.

Olding, Frank. (2024). *The Taliesin Sourcebook*. Green Magic.

Parker, Will. (2005). *The four branches of the Mabinogi*. Oregon House, Ca: Bardic Press.

Rekdal, Jan Erik and Doherty, C. (2016). *King and warrior in early north-west Europe*. Dublin: Four Courts Press.

Roberts, B.F. (1988). *Early Welsh poetry: studies in the Book of Aneirin ed. by Brynley F. Roberts*. Aberystwyth: National Library of Wales.

Sheehan, Sarah. (2009). Matrilineal Subjects: Ambiguity, Bodies, and Metamorphosis in the Fourth Branch of the Mabinogi. *Signs: Journal of Women in Culture and Society*, 34(2), pp.319–342. doi:https://doi.org/10.1086/591089

Starling, Mhara. (2022). *Welsh Witchcraft*. Llewellyn Worldwide.

Sullivan, Charles WM. (1996). *The Mabinogi: a book of essays*. New York: Garland Pub.

Thomas, Gwyn. (1976). *Y traddodiad barddol*. Gwasg Prifysgol Cymru.

Tolstoy, Nikolai. (2010). *The oldest British prose literature: the compilation of the four branches of the Mabinogi*. Lewiston, N.Y.; Lampeter: Edwin Mellen Press.

Williams, Ifor. (1996). *Pedeir keinc y Mabinogi: allan o Lyfr Gwyn Rhydderch*. Caerdydd: Gwasg Prifysgol Cymru.

Williams, Mark. (2021). *The Celtic Myths that Shape the Way We Think*. Thames & Hudson.

Zeiser, Sarah. (2010). Performing a Literary Paternity Test: Bonedd yr Arwyr and the Fourth Branch of the Mabinogi. *Proceedings of the Harvard Celtic Colloquium*, 28(2008).

About the Author

Kristoffer Hughes is founder and head of the Anglesey Druid Order, he is a member of the Order of Bards, Ovates and Druids, and a Druid member of the Gorsedd of Wales. He is an award-winning author of several titles that focus on Celtic and Welsh mythology, death, dying and bereavement. He leads workshops and courses online and in person throughout the UK, Europe, the USA and Australia. You can contact him by searching for Kristoffer Hughes on Facebook, and also by going to angleseydruidorder.co.uk

MOON BOOKS

PAGANISM & SHAMANISM

What is Paganism? A religion, a spirituality, an alternative belief system, nature worship? You can find support for all these definitions (and many more) in dictionaries, encyclopedias, and text books of religion, but subscribe to any one and the truth will evade you. Above all Paganism is a creative pursuit, an encounter with reality, an exploration of meaning and an expression of the soul. Druids, Heathens, Wiccans and others, all contribute their insights and literary riches to the Pagan tradition. Moon Books invites you to begin or to deepen your own encounter, right here, right now.

If you have enjoyed this book, why not tell other readers by posting a review on your preferred book site.

Bestsellers from Moon Books
Pagan Portals Series

The Morrigan
Meeting the Great Queens
Morgan Daimler
Ancient and enigmatic, the Morrigan reaches out to us. On shadowed wings and in raven's call, meet the ancient Irish goddess of war, battle, prophecy, death, sovereignty, and magic.
Paperback: 978-1-78279-833-0 ebook: 978-1-78279-834-7

The Awen Alone
Walking the Path of the Solitary Druid
Joanna van der Hoeven
An introductory guide for the solitary Druid, The Awen Alone will accompany you as you explore, and seek out your own place within the natural world.
Paperback: 978-1-78279-547-6 ebook: 978-1-78279-546-9

Moon Magic
Rachel Patterson
An introduction to working with the phases of the Moon, what they are and how to live in harmony with the lunar year and to utilise all the magical powers it provides.
Paperback: 978-1-78279-281-9 ebook: 978-1-78279-282-6

Hekate
A Devotional
Vivienne Moss
Hekate, Queen of Witches and the Shadow-Lands, haunts the pages of this devotional bringing magic and enchantment into your lives.
Paperback: 978-1-78535-161-7 ebook: 978-1-78535-162-4

Bestsellers from Moon Books

Keeping Her Keys

An Introduction to Hekate's Modern Witchcraft

Cyndi Brannen

Blending Hekate, witchcraft and personal development together to create a powerful new magickal perspective.

Paperback: 978-1-78904-075-3 ebook 978-1-78904-076-0

Journey to the Dark Goddess

How to Return to Your Soul

Jane Meredith

Discover the powerful secrets of the Dark Goddess and transform your depression, grief and pain into healing and integration.

Paperback: 978-1-84694-677-6 ebook: 978-1-78099-223-5

Shamanic Reiki

Expanded Ways of Working with Universal Life Force Energy

Llyn Roberts, Robert Levy

Shamanism and Reiki are each powerful ways of healing; together, their power multiplies. Shamanic Reiki introduces techniques to help healers and Reiki practitioners tap ancient healing wisdom.

Paperback: 978-1-84694-037-8 ebook: 978-1-84694-650-9

Southern Cunning

Folkloric Witchcraft in the American South

Aaron Oberon

Modern witchcraft with a Southern flair, this book is a journey through the folklore of the American South and a look at the power these stories hold for modern witches.

Paperback: 978-1-78904-196-5 ebook: 978-1-78904-197-2